Introducing
Religious Ethics

Dilwyn Hunt

Nelson Thornes

...siness

09.2009

Published in 2007 by:
Nelson Thornes Ltd
Delta Place
27 Bath Road
CHELTENHAM
GL53 7TH
United Kingdom

07 08 09 10 11 / 10 9 8 7 6 5 4 3 2 1

A catalogue record for this book is available from the British Library

ISBN 978 0 7487 8445 5

Cover illustration by Ian West
Illustrations by Ian West
Page make-up by eMC Design
Picture Research by Sue Sharp

Printed and bound in Croatia by Zrinski

Acknowledgements

Alamy/ Alan McIntyre: 59; Alamy/ Arkreligion.com: 10 (top), 17 (top); Alamy/ BE&W agencja fotograficzna Sp. z o.o.: 51 (bottom); Alamy/ Ben Molyneux:
48 (bottom); Alamy/ Bubbles Photo Library: 66 (bottom); Alamy/ Chris Rout: 31 (right); Alamy/ Janine Wiedel Photolibrary: 76 (bottom); Alamy/ Martin
Lee: 71 (bottom); Alamy/ Medical-on-line: 6 (top); Alamy/ plainpicture GmbH & Co. kg: 39; Alamy/ Popperfoto: 12 (bottom left); Alamy/ Profimedia
International s.r.o: 53; Alamy/ Rob Walls: 20 (bottom), 55 (bottom); Alamy/ Roger Bamber: 69 (top), 74 (bottom); Alamy/ Simon Grosset: 44 (top), 46
(middle); Alamy/ Stan Kujawa: 30 (bottom); Alamy/ Stephen Oliver: 52 (bottom); Alamy/ The Print Collector: 4, 7 (middle); Alamy/ Visual Arts Library
(London): 1 (top); Ancient Art & Architecture Collection Ltd: 1 (bottom), 7 (top); Art Archive/ Malmaison Musée du Chateau/ Alfredo Dagli Orti: 40 (top);
The Arthur Szyk Society: 13 (bottom), Brand X Pictures (NT): 13 (top right); Bridgeman Art Library/ John Stuart Mill (1806-73) 1973 (oil on canvas),
Watts, George Frederick (1817-1904) / © Trustees of the Watts Gallery, Compton, Surrey, UK: 45, 46 (bottom); Bridgeman Art Library/ Master Isaac
Newton, 1905 (oil on canvas), Hannah, Robert (1812-1909) /The Royal Institution, London, UK: 32 (top); Bridgeman Art Library/ Portrait of Aristotle
(384-322 BC), c.1475 (oil on panel), Joos van Gent (Joos van Wassenhove) (fl.1460-75)/ Louvre, Paris, France, Giraudon: 15 (top), 17 (bottom),
21; Bridgeman Art Library/ Portrait of Benjamin Constant de Rebecque (1767-1830) (oil on canvas), Roches, Hercule de (fl.1856)/ Musee de la Vie
Romantique, Paris, France, Lauros / Giraudon: 34 (top); Bridgeman Art Library/ Portrait of Emmanuel Kant (1724-1804) (oil on canvas), German School,
(18th century)/ Private Collection: 30 (top), 36 (top left), 37 (top); Bridgeman Art Library/ St Thomas Aquinas (1225-1274), Bartolommeo, Fra (Baccio
della Porta) (1472-1517)/ Museo di San Marco dell'Angelico, Florence, Italy: 22 (bottom); Bridgeman Art Library/ Survivors from a shipwreck off the Isle
of Wight being rescued by the crew of H.M.S. Juno, Dodd, Robert (1748-1815)/ Private Collection, Photo © Bonhams, London: 56 (top); Bridgeman Art
Library/ The Kiss of Judas, 1442 (fresco), Angelico, Fra (Guido di Pietro) (c.1387-1455)/ Museo di San Marco dell'Angelico, Florence, Italy: 54 (right);
Bridgeman Art Library/ The Washing of the Feet, 1500 (oil on panel), Lodi, Giovanni Agostino da (fl.1490-1520)/ Galleria dell' Accademia, Venice, Italy,
Cameraphoto Arte Venezia: 49 (top); Corbis: 15 (bottom), 35 (top); Corbis/ Araldo de Luca: 68 (bottom), 74 (top); Corbis/ Art Archive: 49 (bottom left);
Corbis/ Bettmann: 16 (both), 76 (top); Corbis/ Chinanews Photo/ Reuters: 66 (top); Corbis/ Gavriel Jecan: 9 (bottom); Corbis/ Ian Hodgson: 62 (bottom);
Corbis/ Kate Mitchell/ Zefa: 72; Corbis/ Philippe Lissac: 64 (top); Corbis/ Pinto: 8 (top); Corel 127 (NT): 23 (left); Corel 427 (NT): 48 (top); Corel 449
(NT): 43, 69 (bottom); Corel 484 (NT): 8 (bottom); Corel 588 (NT): 38 (bottom); Corel 654 (NT): 24 (bottom); Corel 675 (NT): 2, 7 (bottom); Digital
Stock 12 (NT) 38 (top); Evangelium Vitae, by the Daughters of St. Paul, Copyright 1995, Daughters of St. Paul. Used by permission of Pauline Books &
Media, 50 St. Paul's Avenue, Boston, MA 02130. All rights reserved: 25 (top), 26 (bottom); Getty Images: 34 (bottom), 36 (bottom), 37 (bottom), 58
(bottom), 61 (bottom); Getty Images/ AFP: 25 (bottom), 51 (top); Getty Images/ Dave Hogan: 18 (right); Getty Images/ Holly Harris: 35 (bottom); Ikon 002
(NT): 28 (bottom); Illustrated London News (NT): 9 (top); Mary Evans Picture Library: 5, 20 (top), 42 (bottom), 44 (bottom), 54 (left), 57, 70; National
Portrait Gallery London: 40 (bottom), 46 (top); New Life Community Church, Stafford, Virginia: 58 (top); Offside Sports Photography: 75 (bottom);
Photodisc 16 (NT): 29 (right); Photodisc 32 (NT): 12 (bottom right), 13 (top left); Photodisc 40 (NT): 28 (top); Punch Ltd, Reproduced with permission
of Punch Ltd.,www.punch.co.uk: 41; Pymca/ Natalie Pecht: 55 (middle); Reuters Picture Library: Philippe Wojazer: 10 (bottom); Rex Features: 75 (top);
Rex Features/ Alexandro Buxbaum: 24 (top right), 26 (middle), 27 (bottom); Rex Features/ Image Source: 29 (left), 32 (bottom), 33 (top), 37 (middle), 71
(top); Rex Features/ Nigel R. Barklie: 61 (left); Rex Features/ Patrick Frillet: 6 (bottom); Rex Features/ Rex Interstock: 31 (left); Rex Features/ Sam Foot:
36 (middle right); Rex Features/ Stuart Clarke: 47; Scala Picture Library: 22 (top); Sonia Halliday Photo Library: 49 (bottom right); Southern Evangelical
Seminary and Bible College NC: 56 (bottom); Still Pictures: 24 (middle left), 63, 65 (middle); Stockpix 5 (NT): 23 (right), 26 (top); Superstock/ age
Fotostock: 19; Topfoto: 62 (top), 65 (top), 67, 68 (middle all); World Religions Photo Library: 64 (bottom), 65 (bottom).

Contents

Religious ethics? What's that then, Mrs Grosvenor? Do you eat it, wear it, download it or plug it in?

Ethics is about right and wrong, Matthew. Religious ethics is about what religions have said on right and wrong.

What is religious ethics?

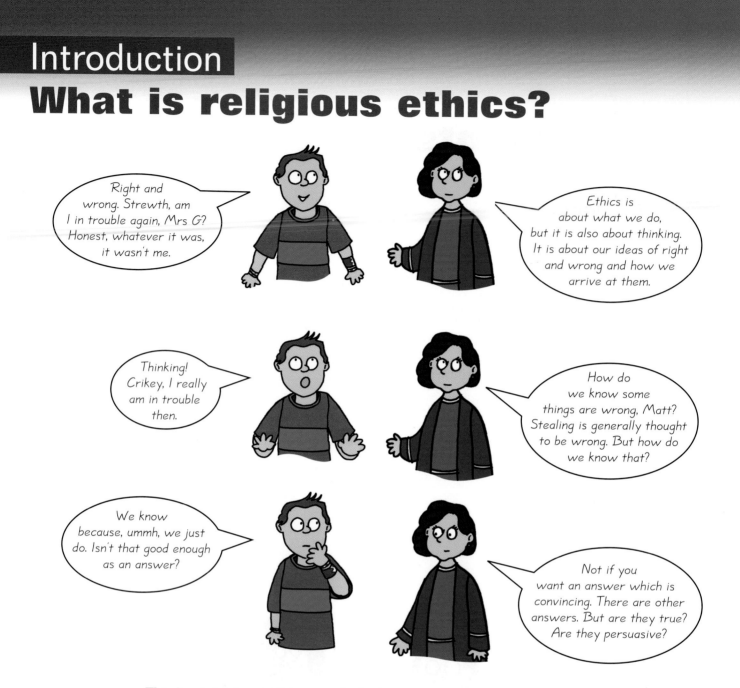

This book is about ethics, particularly religious ethics. It is about the different ways in which religions have answered questions about what is right and wrong. Ethics is a branch of philosophy. Sometimes it is called moral philosophy. This book is a follow-up to *Introducing Philosophy of Religion*. You don't have to have read that book to understand this one, but it would help.

All the world's great religions have something to say about right and wrong. Some religions have rules about stealing, cruelty, sharing or the use of force. These rules are called ethical rules. Often they are called moral rules. Today the words 'ethical' and 'moral' have a similar meaning. There are many sentences where 'moral' can be substituted for 'ethical', and vice versa, without changing the meaning.

UNIVERSITY OF CHICHESTER

For thousands of years humans have thought about right and wrong. They have asked questions like:

- How do we know right from wrong?
- Is there a clear way of knowing that something is right or wrong?
- Is right and wrong just a personal matter?
- Is it God that decides what is right and wrong?

This book looks at some of the ideas people have developed while trying to answer such questions. In particular, it looks at some of the moral theories and beliefs that religions teach. The book explores questions like:

- Do these moral theories make sense?
- What reasons are used to support these theories?
- Are these reasons convincing?
- Do these reasons stand up to scrutiny?

We can all think ethically. We are all able to be moral philosophers. In a sense, we can't avoid being moral philosophers. No one can go through life without making moral decisions. Daily, how we respond to people around us, or even how we treat other living creatures, forces us into making moral choices, whether we like it or not.

How we make those choices is often very much up to us. Is our moral thinking flawed in a way that we don't realise? Or is our moral thinking consistent and well reasoned? Moral thinking isn't just a pastime for old boffins with nothing better to do. All of us have to learn to think morally. And when we do think morally, it is better that we do it well rather than badly.

Unit 1
Divine command theory

How do we know what is right and wrong? Billions of people have a straightforward answer to this question. What is right and wrong is decided by God. If God commands that something is wrong, then it is wrong. If God commands that something is good, then it is good. This is known as the **divine command theory**. The word 'divine' comes from a Latin word for God. The divine command theory has been around for thousands of years. In fact, the idea is so old, it is impossible to say who first suggested it or how it came about.

Perhaps the best-known thinker that believed in the divine command theory was William of Ockham. William of Ockham was born in England in about 1285. He was a Christian friar who taught at Oxford and went on to live in France and later in Germany. He wrote in Latin and used many technical words which are difficult to translate. But put simply his view was something like this.

Divine command theory

God is Lord of everything. As Lord of everything, God must also be Lord over what is good. There isn't a separate standard called 'good' against which God can be measured.
If such a separate standard of 'good' existed, it could be used to judge whether God really was 'good'. Such a standard would make 'good' a sort of judge over God. But 'good' cannot be a judge over God. What is 'good' is decided by God. Good and bad are whatever God commands.

William of Ockham (c. 1285–1349)
'The will of God is the sovereign arbiter of moral good or evil.'

Activity 1 Does God decide?

Discuss the following statement in a group of three:

What is right and wrong is decided by God.

Do you agree or disagree with this statement? Give your reasons and report back on your discussion to the whole class.

Activity 2 Is Ockham's argument persuasive?

With a partner study William of Ockham's argument. Notice in particular how it begins.

a How has Ockham tried to make the argument persuasive?

b Is the argument true or are there obvious flaws or weaknesses?

A horse and cart argument

An argument can be structured in many ways. Perhaps the simplest way of structuring an argument is the horse and cart argument. A horse and cart always has three parts: (1) a horse, (2) a harness and (3) a cart. These three parts are always placed in the same order.

— (1) A horse

— (2) A harness, or a connecting device

— (3) A cart

The horse and cart argument also has three basic parts: (1) an opinion, (2) a connective and (3) a **reason**. These three parts are also usually placed in the same order. First the presenter of the argument begins with an opinion. This is a statement of what the presenter

Moses and God's commandments

In the Bible there are several passages which seem to support the divine command theory. Perhaps the most famous is the story of God giving his commandments to Moses. The story is over 3,000 years old.

God gives his commandments

After helping the Hebrew people to escape from slavery, God tells their leader Moses to climb Mount Sinai. Somewhere near the top of the mountain, God appears to Moses. In what seems to have been an amazing experience, God gives his commandments to Moses. God speaks each commandment out loud and writes them onto two stone tablets. At the end of the story, the Bible says, 'When he had finished speaking with Moses on Mount Sinai, the Lord gave him the two tablets of stone written with the finger of God' (Exodus Ch 31 v 18).

Tradition has it that the Ten Commandments were engraved on the stone tablets. Many Christians and some Jews believe that it is essential to obey these ten laws in order to live a good life.

Moses shows the people the stone tablets on which God's commandments are written.

'Written with the finger of God.' That sure looks to me as if God is telling us what is right and wrong.

Perhaps, but is that the only way of understanding those words,

The Ten Commandments

(Exodus Ch 20 v 1–17)

You shall have no gods before me.

Do not make a carved image to worship.

Do not misuse God's name.

Keep the Sabbath day holy.

Honour your father and mother.

You shall not kill.

You shall not commit adultery.

You shall not steal.

You shall not bear false witness.

You shall not covet your neighbour's belongings.

Is God the author of moral values?

Divine command theory

The story of the Ten Commandments does seem to support the divine command theory. The words 'written with the finger of God' do look like a clear claim that God is the author of **moral** values.

However, is that the only way in which the words can be understood? It may mean that God **recognises** what is good and is **recommending** what is good to all of us in the form of a clear set of dos and don'ts. What is 'good' is, as Plato believed, above and beyond God's control. God may, however, know what is 'good' and may be giving out commands which are in line with what is 'good'.

The answer to all moral problems?

The Ten Commandments appear to provide what looks like a very clear set of moral rules. 'You shall not kill', 'You shall not steal', what could be more straightforward? However, do the Ten Commandments answer all of our moral problems?

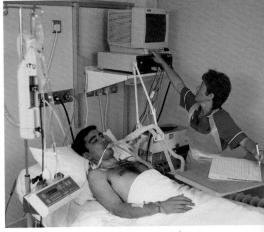

For example, the commandment, 'You shall not kill' means taking the life of an innocent person is wrong. But does it also mean that fighting to defend your country is also wrong? Does it mean that the death penalty for a person found guilty of murder is wrong? For many people, far from providing clear answers, the Ten Commandments seem to leave many moral problems unanswered.

Turning off a life-support system that is keeping an apparently brain-dead patient alive – is it right or wrong?

Activity 4 Ten Commandments

To live a life that is good, we only have to keep the Ten Commandments

Do you agree or disagree with this statement? Explain your answer.

In the religion of Judaism these problems are partly answered by the claim that Moses was not given just the Ten Commandments. In Judaism the belief has been that God gave Moses 613 written commandments. Along with the written commandments, Moses was also given teaching from God as to what the commandments meant. This extra teaching is called the **oral tradition** and is said to have been passed on to the prophets and teachers that came after Moses.

However, with so many commandments, doesn't that just make answering moral problems more difficult? Isn't there a single rule, a golden rule, which can provide an answer to most moral problems?

Killing locusts to protect your crops – is it right or wrong?

Ockham's argument

William of Ockham's argument for divine command theory can be put as follows:

- God is Lord of everything.
- God is Lord of what is good and bad.
- Good and bad are whatever God commands.

William of Ockham's theory claims that if there wasn't a God, it would be impossible for us to know what 'good' is. In fact, 'good' wouldn't exist in a godless world.

Plato and divine command theory

- What is good is an unchanging truth which even God cannot change.
- God commands that some things are good because they are good in themselves.
- Things are not good because God has given a command saying that they are good.

Plato believed that 'the good' stood above and beyond God's control. Humans can know what is good independently of God, but this requires wisdom and patient study.

Structuring an argument

A horse and cart argument

The simplest way of structuring an argument is a horse and cart argument. This involves having (1) an opinion, (2) a connective and (3) a reason. Arguments of this kind are coherent but often they are not very interesting or very persuasive.

A pyramid argument

A pyramid argument is founded on a statement which a lot of people are likely to agree with, particularly members of your predicted audience. Additional statements are made which seem to follow on from the opening statement and that lead to a final conclusion.

Unit 1 Things to do

Activity 5 Moral problems today

Working in a group of three or four, describe the most significant moral problems which young people most frequently have to deal with.

Avoid simply making a list such as mobile phone theft, tidying up your bedroom, bullying.

Provide enough information to make it clear why the issue is a moral problem.

Activity 6 Flattering the audience

Sometimes the answer to an issue is stated but a proper proof is glossed over. The glossing over may be attempted by trying to flatter or lull the audience into agreeing that the answer is already known. This statement is an example:

All reasonable people know that nuclear weapons are a waste of money.

As most people like to think of themselves as reasonable, disagreeing seems out of the question.

Look at the following statements and decide which ones are trying to flatter the audience into agreement:

a Shoplifting is a crime we all have to pay for in higher shop prices.

b The latest figures show that nearly 40% of marriages in Britain end in divorce.

c Everyone knows that violent computer games make young people violent.

d All fair-minded people realise that animals have rights just like humans.

e None of us are perfect, we all make mistakes.

f Any intelligent person knows that genetically modified crops are bad for you.

g Around the world there are still animals in zoos that are being kept in unacceptable conditions.

h It's a well-known fact that over the past 30 years the moral standards of young people have gone down.

i It's generally agreed that illegal immigrants live off benefits.

j Street crime is still a significant problem in Britain.

Activity 7 Continuum

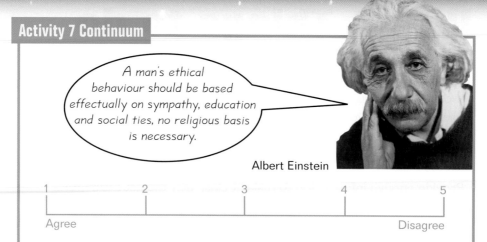

> A man's ethical behaviour should be based effectually on sympathy, education and social ties, no religious basis is necessary.

Albert Einstein

1	2	3	4	5

Agree   Disagree

a Do you agree or disagree with Einstein's claim that you don't have to be religious to be an ethical person?

On a scale of 1 to 5, rate your response and write your number on a piece of paper. Place all the papers into a box and shake them up. Have everyone take out one of the papers. Ask everyone with number 1 to form a line so as to make a human bar chart. Do the same for 2, 3, 4 and 5.

b Brainstorm reasons or ideas which support the statement and which don't support the statement. Working with a partner, produce an argument to support the statement or reject the statement.

Avoid using a basic horse and cart argument; try to write a pyramid argument.

Activity 8 A class debate

Organise a formal class debate. In teams of four, choose a motion to debate; you could use one of the suggested motions (a) to (e) or develop a motion of your own.

You need one team to propose each motion and one team to oppose each notion. Suggest a time limit for each speech of 1–2 minutes.

a This house believes that what is right and what is wrong is just a matter of opinion.

b This house believes that there are certain things which everyone knows are good and certain things which everyone knows are evil.

c This house believes that to inflict pain on a guinea pig is just as bad as inflicting pain on a human being.

d This house believes that lying is always wrong and is never justified.

e This house believes that around the world there are still animals in zoos that are being kept in unacceptable conditions.

The Golden Rule

Not long after Jesus began teaching, Matthew's Gospel says that Jesus went up a mountain and his disciples gathered around him. Jesus then preached a sermon. This sermon is called the **Sermon on the Mount**. It is thought by many to contain some of the most significant things Jesus ever said on the subject of moral behaviour.

'Always treat others as you would like them to treat you; that is the meaning of the Law and the Prophets.'

A second Moses

Many people have thought that there is a similarity between Moses giving out God's commandments on a mountain and Jesus also giving out his ethical teaching on a mountain. Jesus may be seen as a second Moses declaring new commandments because a new age had arrived. Yet Jesus, it appears, claimed that he had not come to replace the law given to Moses, but rather he had come to 'fulfil the law'.

Towards the end of his sermon, Jesus boldly declares that all of the laws given to Moses, including the Ten Commandments, and all of the **oral tradition** passed on to Moses and the Prophets can be summed up in a single rule: 'Treat others as you would like them to treat you.'

God's ultimate moral law?

'Treat others as you would like them to treat you' is known as the **Golden Rule**. Some people believe that the Golden Rule is God's ultimate moral law, a sort of eleventh commandment which rules over all the other commandments.

However, the Golden Rule doesn't appear to rely on a belief in God, or on holy scripture or a religious leader. The rule, it is claimed, is a non-religious principle which anyone can use. For example, Peter Tatchell is a human rights campaigner who over 30 years ago abandoned religious **faith**. Today he says, 'I try to live by the **maxim**: treat others as you would like them to treat you. This is not a religious philosophy; it is common sense and human decency.'

Peter Tatchell
'I try to live by the maxim: Treat others as you would like them to treat you.'

What does the Golden Rule mean?

The Golden Rule is based on the idea of giving to other people what you would want for yourself. Behind the rule is the belief that most of the time you get back what you give out. If you are selfish and mean, you can expect people to be selfish and mean towards you. If you are helpful and fair, you can expect people to be helpful and fair in return. The rule is often put to people in the form of a question: How would you feel if someone did that to you?

The tit for tat rule

The Golden Rule is not the same as tit for tat. Tit for tat simply means that if a person treats you badly, then treat them equally badly. This is the law of **retaliation**, or **lex talionis** in Latin. For some people, tit for tat can have a positive side to it, so that if a person is considerate to you, be considerate towards them.

With the Golden Rule, the idea is to be fair and considerate towards all people all of the time, even if they are not very fair to you, because being considerate is how you would want to be treated.

How does the Golden Rule work?

Perhaps the best way to understand the Golden Rule is to think about how it would work in a real situation. For example, how might the Golden Rule be used in the case of Shanice and Jade?

Shanice and Jade do not get on. They are both aged about 11 and live quite close to each other. Jade is always rude to Shanice. She never plays with Shanice or offers a friendly word. Shanice is never rude to Jade and doesn't shout back.

One day Shanice sees Jade sitting on her front doorstep. Jade has a cut on her knee and her elbow is bleeding. Shanice asks her if she is okay. 'Are you stupid?' Jade replies, fighting back the tears, 'The chain on my bike broke and I fell off. My mum's gone out and I can't get into the house.'

Activity 1 Using the Golden Rule

If Shanice followed the Golden Rule, how might the story end? Explain your answer.

The story might end in many different ways, but here is one possible ending:

Shanice gets some warm water and some bandages. She helps Jade clean her cuts. Shanice also helps Jade to pick up her bike and put it away in the garage. She brings Jade a can of drink and a sandwich and asks Jade if she wants to sit in her house while she waits for her mum to come back. Jade refuses. After a while, Jade's mum comes back and Jade goes inside her house.

Shanice knows that if she came off her bike and injured herself, she would hope someone would help her out. That's how she would want to be treated in that situation. So, when Shanice sees Jade hurt, she helps Jade and treats her as she herself would want to be treated.

Activity 2 People can't be that good

Do you agree or disagree with this statement?

The Golden Rule is unrealistic as it expects people to be too good.

Have a discussion in groups of three or four. Report back on your discussion to the rest of the class.

An ancient moral law?

Jesus wasn't the first or the only religious leader to propose the Golden Rule. Many of the world's great religions, such as Confucianism, Buddhism, Hinduism, Judaism and Islam, have a tradition of their religious leaders or founders teaching the Golden Rule. For some, this widespread use suggests that it forms a sort of universal moral law which all can agree on.

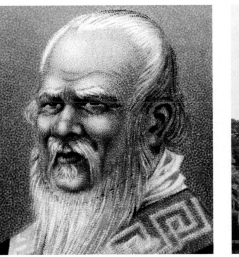

Confucianism
'What one does not wish for oneself, one ought not to do to anyone else' (Confucius, 551–479 BCE).

Buddhism
'Hurt not others in ways that you yourself would find hurtful' (Gotama the Buddha, 563–483 BCE).

Hinduism
'One should not behave towards others in a way which is disagreeable to oneself. This is the essence of morality' (*The Mahabharata*).

Islam
'Not one of you is truly a believer until he wishes for his brother what he wishes for himself' (Muhammad the Prophet, 570–632 CE).

Judaism
'That which is hateful to you, do not do to your neighbour. That is the whole of the Law, the rest is commentary' (Hillel the Elder, c. 70 BCE to 10 CE).

It is very likely that Jesus heard a version of the Golden Rule when he was a small boy as part of the law given to Moses. In the Jewish Bible it says, 'You shall not seek revenge, you shall love your neighbour like yourself' (Leviticus Ch 19 v 18).

It is also quite likely that Jesus would have known about Hillel the Elder's version of the Golden Rule. Hillel was one of the most famous of all Jewish teachers. He was teaching at about the time when Jesus was born. Like many others, Hillel said that the Golden Rule neatly summed up his ethical teaching. Hillel's Golden Rule was:

> That which is hateful to you, do not do to your neighbour. That is the whole of the Law, the rest is commentary.

The negative Golden Rule

Jesus' Golden Rule begins 'Always treat others …'. This is often called the **positive Golden Rule** as it requires taking positive action for the sake of others. It is sometimes compared with the **negative Golden Rule**. Hillel the Elder, for example, is often claimed to have provided a negative Golden Rule when he said, 'That which is hateful to you, do not do to your neighbour.' Hillel's rule, it is suggested, doesn't say do things for the sake of others. It merely says don't do anything hateful. But is that being fair to Hillel?

Activity 3 Two rules, one outcome?

With a partner study Jesus' Golden Rule and compare it with Hillel the Elder's Golden Rule.

That which is hateful to you, do not do to your neighbour. (Hillel the Elder)	Always treat others as you would like them to treat you. (Jesus)

a Try out these two rules using the story of Shanice and Jade.

b Do the two rules give the same answer or different answers? Explain your thinking.

The Silver Rule

A number of the great religious leaders of the past claimed that the Golden Rule summed up their moral teaching. However, they didn't claim that it answered all moral problems.

One criticism of the Golden Rule is that 'treating others as you would like them to treat you' doesn't take into account different people's likes and dislikes. Sometimes people don't want to be treated in the way **you** want to be treated. Sometimes they want to be treated in the way **they** want to be treated.

I know you are trying to be helpful, but I don't want your help. Please leave me alone.

In the story of Shanice and Jade, suppose Shanice decides to help Jade. But Jade makes it clear she doesn't want any help. If Shanice carries on and ignores what Jade says, wouldn't that be disrespectful to Jade and be wrong? Don't we have to listen to people and take account of what they say they want? Isn't it wrong to carry on giving a person help, ignoring what they say they want?

This criticism of the Golden Rule leads to another moral principle called the **Silver Rule**. The Silver Rule is, 'Treat others as they wish to be treated.'

But if the Golden Rule doesn't work all of the time, how do you know when it is right to use it?

Does it answer the moral problem 'Should my mum keep telling me to tidy up my bedroom?'

It seems to work well when basic human rights or needs are the issue.

The Golden Rule can also give a sense of reason to a moral argument. A moral argument doesn't have to be just an appeal to emotions. A moral argument can be a balanced argument.

A balanced argument

A **balanced argument** is often thought of as being one where both sides of the argument are explored before deciding which to support. It shows that a person is knowledgeable of both views and that they are willing to consider a view which opposes their own.

Aristotle (384–322 BCE)
'The arousing of prejudice, pity, anger and similar emotions has nothing to do with the essential facts.'

However, an argument can be balanced in a quite different way. An argument can be balanced in the sense that it is level-headed and reasonable. The tone of the argument is sensible and calm and the presenter of the argument comes across as a person who is sane, not hysterical and shows good judgement.

The great Greek philosopher Aristotle wrote about how a persuasive argument should be based on reason, or **logos**. However, he also recognised that people's minds were not likely to be changed by a cold, logical argument. Aristotle knew that appealing to people's emotions and feelings, what Aristotle called **pathos**, could also be important. However, according to Aristotle, an argument that was overly full of pathos and that lacked balance was little more than an attempt to persuade by trickery.

A balanced argument, then, has a calm tone. It tries to avoid using language which is unnecessarily emotive. It doesn't make exaggerated claims in an attempt to raise strong feelings like anger or fear. A balanced argument should appeal to people's reason.

A great civil rights speech

In 1963 there were parts of America where local laws made it legal to ban black people from restaurants and schools. John F. Kennedy, who was then America's president, was anxious to get rid of these laws.

But Kennedy knew that simply changing the law wasn't enough. He had to convince many Americans that it was wrong to treat people differently because of their skin colour.

On 11 June 1963 Kennedy decided to go on TV to speak to the entire nation.

John F. Kennedy
'This is one country. It has become one country because all of us and all the people who came here had an equal chance to develop their talents.'

Activity 4 Choose a speech

With the help of his speech-writers, imagine Kennedy ends up with two versions of his speech, version 1 and version 2.

A complete version of the original speech may be read and heard on www.americanrhetoric.com/speeches/jfkcivilrights.htm.

a In order to convince his audience, which one do you think he should use? Explain why.

b Which one of these versions makes most effective use of the Golden Rule? Give your reasons.

c Which of these versions makes best use of a balanced and calm tone? Explain your answer.

Version 1

Good evening, my fellow citizens.
We are confronted primarily with a moral issue. It is as old as the Scriptures and is as clear as the American Constitution.

The heart of the question is whether all Americans are to have equal rights, whether we are going to treat our fellow Americans as we want to be treated.

If an American, because his skin is dark, cannot eat in a restaurant open to the public, if he cannot send his children to the best school available, if he cannot vote for the public officials who will represent him, if, in short, he cannot enjoy the full and free life which all of us want, then who among us would be content to have the colour of his skin changed and stand in his place? Who among us would then be content with advice saying be patient, not yet?

Version 2

Good evening, everyone.
We are confronted primarily with a moral issue. It is as old as the Rocky Mountains and as clear as a mountain stream.

The heart of the question is whether all people in this country are to have equal rights and whether white racists are to be allowed to abuse black people.

If in this country, because a person's skin is dark they are humiliated by not being allowed to eat in a restaurant open to the public, if his children are treated as lepers and can't go to the best school available, if he cannot even be given the common decency of being allowed to vote for the public official he wants, then why shouldn't he get angry and say, 'Enough is enough, things have to change now'? Every sensible person knows that racism is wrong and disgusting, so let's put a stop to it now.

Demonstrators in 1957 attempt to stop black students attending an American university.

Black demonstrators in 1960 are refused service at a 'whites only' lunch counter.

The Golden Rule

Treat others as you would like them to treat you.

- A version of the Golden Rule is found in most of the world's great religions.
- The Golden Rule is based on the idea of giving to other people what you would want for yourself.
- The rule is often put to people in the form of a question: How would you feel if someone did that to you?
- The Golden Rule is not the same as tit for tat.

The negative Golden Rule

That which is hateful to you, do not do to your neighbour.

- The positive Golden Rule requires taking positive action for the sake of others. The negative Golden Rule is often seen as less demanding as it only requires not doing anything hateful.

The Silver Rule

Treat others as they wish to be treated.

- The Silver Rule is used to cope with the claim that sometimes people don't want to be treated in the way you want to be treated. Sometimes they want to be treated in the way they want to be treated.

A balanced argument

- A balanced argument can be one where both sides of the argument are explored before deciding which to support.
- A balanced argument can also be an argument that is level-headed and reasonable.
- The tone of a balanced argument is sensible and calm.
- A balanced argument appeals to people's reason and is not unnecessarily emotive.

Aristotle (384–322 BCE)

18

Unit 2 Things to do

Activity 5 Useful words

The boxes contain two words often used when talking about moral behaviour.

retaliation	principles

What do these words mean? Choose the word which best completes each speech bubble. Make up a sentence of your own using one of the two words.

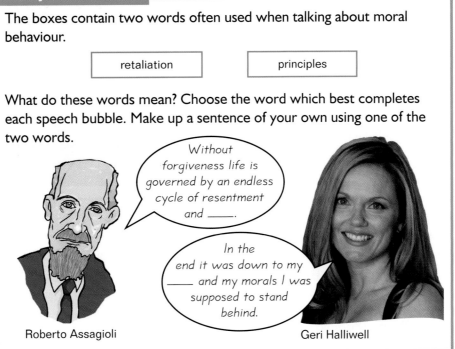

Without forgiveness life is governed by an endless cycle of resentment and ____.

Roberto Assagioli

In the end it was down to my ____ and my morals I was supposed to stand behind.

Geri Halliwell

Activity 6 Using the Golden Rule

Gary and Dylan are having a kick-about. Alan, who lives in the same street, shows up and asks if he can join in.

Gary

Dylan

Can I play as well?

Alan

Nah! It's better with just two playing.

It's okay with me, Dylan, if he plays.

Nah! Come on let's play.

a In the story, who do you think should use the Golden Rule – Dylan, Alan, Gary or all three? Explain your answer.

b Does the Golden Rule give a clear answer in this situation? Explain your answer.

c Discuss with a partner any strengths or weaknesses you think the Golden Rule may have. Share your views with the rest of the class.

Activity 7 Logos and pathos

Rewrite the following argument to give it a more reasoned and less emotional tone.

Storekeepers who sell drink to children that are underage are wicked and stupid. Why can't people see sense? Young people who drink think it makes them look grown up but that's just being dumb. Binge drinking is a silly thing to do and people who do it just fall about the streets, looking like clowns and throwing up. One day they will be so drunk they will walk into the road and, smack, a bus will flatten them into the tarmac with blood everywhere. Or else they will end up as a slob on a park bench, desperate for alcohol.

Activity 8 Tit for tat

a Which of the following statements advises retaliation or tit for tat?

   i Treat others as they wish to be treated.
   ii Treat others as you would like them to treat you.
   iii Treat others as they treat you.
   iv Treat others so as to cause no harm.

b The story of Shanice and Jade – how might it have ended if Shanice had followed the tit for tat rule?

c Discuss with a partner any strengths or weaknesses the tit for tat rule may have.

Does the Golden Rule cope with problems today like global warming?

Does the Golden Rule expect us to be too good?

Is the Golden Rule only worth following if everyone does?

Activity 9 Community of enquiry

What question or issue does the Golden Rule raise for you?

a Working in pairs, decide which question or questions you think should be followed up.

b Compare your ideas with another pair and decide, as a group of four, which question should be kept. Fix your questions to a display board. Arrange for everyone to view the suggestions.

c Together as a class, decide which questions should be followed up or discussed further.

Natural law theory

Do moral laws change depending on where you live? This question was argued over by philosophers in ancient Greece 2,500 years ago.

Clothing in ancient Greece   Clothing in ancient Persia

Some Greek philosophers claimed that moral laws were just local conventions. What was wrong in Persia might not be wrong for people who lived in Greece. Just as views about how you should dress or what you should eat varied depending on local customs, the moral law changed depending on where you lived. The belief that all moral laws are just local conventions and that they change depending on what you personally think, is often called **moral relativism**.

However, some of the greatest Greek philosophers, like Plato and Aristotle, argued that moral laws are absolute and unchanging. They believed that wherever you went in the world, these moral laws always stayed the same. The belief that moral laws don't vary from person to person, or place to place, is called **moral objectivism**.

Natural law

Aristotle, in particular, was impressed by what he saw as **objective** laws of nature which never changed. Wood burns in Greece and wood also burns in Persia. Throw a pebble into a river in Greece and it will sink. Throw a pebble into a river in Persia and it too will sink.

Aristotle believed that there are permanent, objective natural laws which govern what will burn and what will float. So also, he believed, there are permanent and objective natural laws which govern what is morally right or wrong.

In *The Nicomachean Ethics*, Aristotle set out his ideas on **ethics** and claimed that all things, including humans, are best governed by these natural laws. Following these natural laws leads to a fulfilled natural end. According to Aristotle, the fulfilled natural end for humans, the ultimate goal of human life, was happiness.

'A law of nature … operates in the same way everywhere – thus fire burns here and in Persia' (Aristotle).

Activity 1 Is right or wrong a personal preference?

Discuss this statement in a group of two or three.

What is right or wrong is all relative; it's just a matter of personal preference.

Do you agree or disagree? Share your discussion with the rest of the class.

Being happy

Aristotle believed that happiness is not the same as having pleasure or a good time. Pleasures of the senses alone do not make us happy. For Aristotle there is no real happiness to be found in being drunk all the time or in being pampered by servants. To find happiness we have to fulfil that part of our nature which makes us different from the other animals. That means we must live in a way which satisfies the highest and noblest part of our nature, our thinking mind.

Aristotle (384–322 BCE)
'Happiness then, the end to which all our conscious acts are directed, is found to be something final and self-sufficient.'

So lying by a swimming pool, under a tropical sun, eating ice cream and chocolate cake every day isn't going to make me happy?

Aristotle didn't think so. What do you think, Matt? What is the secret to being happy?

Activity 2 The secret of happiness

Discuss with a partner how you might complete the statement

The secret to being happy is …

Write down your first thoughts about what 'being happy' means and how it can be achieved. Attach your ideas to a display board to create a class thought wall.

The humanistic tradition

Aristotle believed that by living according to the natural law we become fulfilled and happy people. An acorn ruled by natural law can become an oak tree and so fulfil its potential in life. In a similar way, if a person decides to live a good life by living according to the natural law, they can achieve their potential and find satisfaction in a life well lived.

These ideas from Greek philosophy, rather than from religion, are part of an ancient tradition of **humanism**. Many people who call themselves humanists don't believe that anything goes when it comes to moral values. Nor do they believe that human life is just pointless existence. They believe life does have a purpose but it doesn't rely on a belief in God. Rather it is to do with human beings striving to live a good life, a virtuous life well lived. These ideas have their origin in what people talked about in ancient Greece, and particularly the views of Aristotle.

Christianity and natural law

Early in the history of Christianity, St Paul also claimed that there was a natural law which should be our moral guide. He set out his ideas in letters, many of which are included in the New Testament.

St Paul taught that everyone should be obedient to God's law. He also taught that God's law wasn't a secret mystery but that people knew God's law quite naturally. Even people that did not believe in one God and who knew nothing about Jesus, nevertheless knew 'by nature what the law requires' (Romans Ch 2 v 14).

St Paul of Tarsus (10 BCE to 65 CE)
'When Gentiles who have not the law do by nature what the law requires … they show that what the law requires is written on their hearts'
(Romans Ch 2 v 14–15).

Activity 3 Do you agree?

Which of these two statements do you agree with more? Explain your answer.

Statement A: Everybody in their hearts knows basically what is right and wrong.

Statement B: With some issues it is very difficult to know what is the right thing to do.

God's natural law

However, the Christian thinker that is most famous for his belief in a natural moral law was a friar who lived about 800 years ago. His name was Thomas Aquinas. Deeply influenced by his Christian faith and by his reading of Aristotle, Thomas Aquinas set out his ideas in his book *Summa Theologica*. His views are put simply in the following way.

Thomas Aquinas (c. 1225–1274)
'All those things to which man has a natural inclination, are naturally apprehended by reason as being good.'

Aquinas' natural law theory

When God created humans, God wanted us to be guided towards the most perfect and highest end which humans could achieve. That highest end is to be with God in heaven. To achieve this, God created humans with a natural inclination built into human nature which would guide humans to that end. The natural law – the law that God prescribed for humans – is built into human nature.

We have natural instincts like the survival instinct, and the instinct to have children and to bring them up. We also have a social instinct which makes us want to be with other human beings and makes us feel lonely if we aren't. These instincts have been built into human nature to morally guide us. Ignoring these natural instincts conflicts with the way God intended us to be and so is morally wrong.

Thomas Aquinas argued that in humans, and in some other animals, a male and a female are bonded together to bring up children. Hence marriage for humans is natural. It is part of the natural law. Anything which damages the bond between a husband and wife, like having an affair and committing adultery, threatens the upbringing of children. Consequently, Aquinas claims, adultery is against the natural law and so it is a sin. For Aquinas, **faith** tells us that adultery is wrong as the Bible says, 'You shall not commit adultery.' But Aquinas believes that adultery is also wrong because **reason** tells us that it is against the natural law.

In nature some male and female animals bond together to help bring up children. Hence, Aquinas argues, a man and a woman joined together in marriage is entirely natural. It is part of the natural law.

Whoa, time out! I need to think about this.

I've got one. Animals don't ride bicycles or use underarm deodorant. Does that mean bikes and deodorant are unnatural and wrong?

You're right, Matt. What questions occur to you about Aquinas' argument?

Okay, think about the argument. Are there any hidden assumptions which need to be questioned?

Activity 4 Questions and uncertainties

Write down a list of all the questions or uncertainties that occur to you about Aquinas' natural law theory. Share your questions and views first with a partner and then in a group of four. Report back on your questions and uncertainties to the rest of the class.

Is there really a natural law?

In the Catholic Church, Thomas Aquinas' ideas are particularly deeply admired. Many people today believe that if something is 'unnatural' it is wrong and if something is 'natural' it is good. However, Aquinas' ideas have been questioned by Christians and by non-Christians.

What did Jesus teach?

One leading Christian critic of natural law theory is Hans Kung. Hans Kung is one of the most respected Catholic scholars alive today. He is also a Catholic priest. He believes that there is no natural law. He supports this claim by pointing out that Jesus never mentions a natural law. Jesus also never justifies any of his teaching by referring to a natural law. Although Jesus talks about natural things like the birds of the air, the lilies of the field and the growth of seeds, he never says that there is a natural law, which tells us what is right and wrong.

Hans Kung (1928–)
'Jesus did not defend any "ethics of natural law".'

What is natural and unnatural?

Having more than one wife doesn't seem at all 'unnatural' in some cultures.

Bertrand Russell was a leading British philosopher during the twentieth century. He was also a fearsome critic of religion. Bertrand Russell suggests that Aquinas' conclusions are 'fixed in advance' as they are really based on traditional Church teaching.

At the heart of Russell's criticism is the claim that what we think is 'natural' may be a 'fixed in advance' judgement as we may take those things with which we are familiar, or those things of which we already approve, to be 'natural'.

For example, Aquinas sees **monogamy** – marriage of one man and one woman – to be the right and 'natural' form of marriage. But what about parts of the world where the custom has been that men may take two or more wives? For people brought up in such a culture, having more than one wife doesn't seem odd or 'unnatural' at all. In fact, having only one wife may seem 'unnatural'.

The Catholic Church and the natural law

In two official documents, *Humanae Vitae* 'Of Human Life' and *Evangelium Vitae* 'The Gospel of Life', the Catholic Church has stated that abortion, euthanasia and 'artificial' contraception are wrong. When forming its view, what the Bible said was obviously very important. However, the Church also claimed that these things were against 'natural law'.

Natural law and euthanasia

Euthanasia or assisted suicide includes a wide range of different situations. The form of euthanasia that many see as being most morally justified is called **voluntary euthanasia**. Typically this involves a person that is near to death and is in great pain. To avoid further suffering, the person in pain repeatedly makes it very clear that they wish to end their life and that they want help to make this happen as painlessly as possible.

Pope John Paul II
'I confirm that euthanasia is a grave violation of the law of God. ... This doctrine is based upon the natural law and upon the written word of God' (*Evangelium Vitae*, para 65, 1995)

The Catholic Church's official view is that all forms of euthanasia, including voluntary euthanasia, are always 'a grave violation of the law of God'. Its case against euthanasia was most clearly stated in *Evangelium Vitae*, published in 1995; the box contains a simple version of the argument it uses to explain why euthanasia is wrong.

The case against euthanasia

Euthanasia violates the law of God as it is the deliberate killing of a human being. It is wrong because euthanasia breaks God's written commandment 'You shall not kill'. This commandment forbids the killing of other people. However, it also forbids the killing of oneself, or killing oneself with the help of others. Euthanasia not only breaks the written commandment of God, it also contradicts the natural law. In every one of us there is a natural survival instinct. A person who says that they want help so they can die is saying something which is unnatural as they are choosing death rather than life.

Euthanasia also damages the natural human desire to live in society, because it damages society itself. This is because euthanasia treats life as a mere 'thing', as if life itself is a commodity to be 'possessed' or 'rejected'. By doing so, euthanasia damages society as it diminishes the value society places on life.

Dying with dignity

For some, faced with incurable and often painful diseases, the natural law argument makes little sense. The survival instinct only makes sense when there remains hope of survival. However, when death is near, rather than using medical knowledge to drag out a few more days or weeks, isn't it more humane to hasten death so that a person can die with dignity?

Diane Pretty

Diane Pretty suffered from motor neurone disease. The disease has no known cure. Although the disease does not affect the mind, it does lead to the slow loss of control over the body. In its advanced stages, Diane Pretty would have been unable to move and unable to hasten her own death. In the final stages of the disease, a person often loses the ability to control their breathing. Afraid of the choking and the pain involved in this final stage, Diane Pretty appealed to the European Court of Human Rights to allow her to end her own life, with help from her husband, when the disease became advanced. Her case was refused.

Diane Pretty said that when her disease became advanced she wished to have help to end her life.

Diane Pretty was admitted into a hospice in 2002. She experienced pain and breathing problems but her medication was increased to the point that she was sedated. A week after being admitted into the hospice, Diane Pretty lapsed into a coma. Two days later she eventually died. Her husband, Brian, said, 'Diane had to go through the one thing she had foreseen and was afraid of – and there was nothing I could do to help.'

Unit 3 Summary

Natural law theory

Thomas Aquinas' argument for natural law theory can be put as follows:

- The natural law – the law that God prescribed for humans – is built into human nature.

- We have natural instincts like the survival instinct, the instinct to have and bring up children, and a social instinct which drives us to want to live in the company of other human beings.

- Living in conflict with the natural law that governs our instincts is unnatural and is morally wrong.

Is there really a natural law?

Hans Kung argued that there is no 'natural law'. Jesus never mentions a 'natural law'. If a 'natural law' exists to guide us, why does Jesus not mention it?

A 'fixed in advance' judgement

What we claim is 'natural' may be a 'fixed in advance' judgement. We may take those things we are familiar with, or those things we already approve of, to be 'natural'.

Euthanasia and natural law

- Euthanasia breaks God's written commandment 'You shall not kill'.

- Euthanasia contradicts the 'natural law'. There is a strong natural survival instinct. A person who says that they want help so they can die is saying something which is unnatural as they are choosing death rather than life.

- Euthanasia treats life as a mere 'thing', as if life itself is merely a commodity to be 'possessed' or 'rejected'. Euthanasia damages society as a whole as it diminishes the value society places on life.

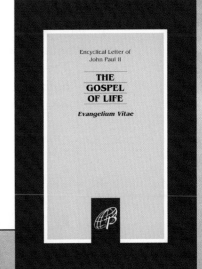

Encyclical Letter of
John Paul II

THE GOSPEL OF LIFE

Evangelium Vitae

Unit 3 Things to do

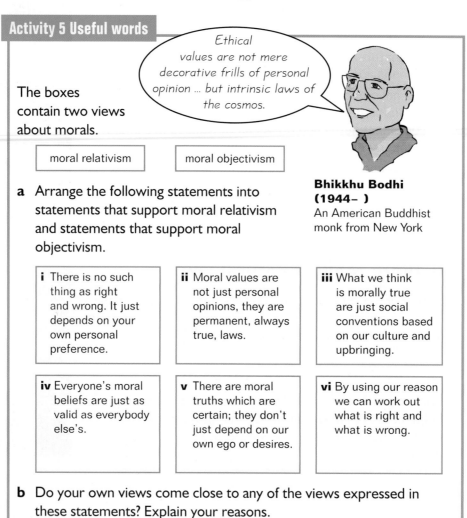

The boxes contain two views about morals.

Ethical values are not mere decorative frills of personal opinion ... but intrinsic laws of the cosmos.

Bhikkhu Bodhi (1944–)
An American Buddhist monk from New York

moral relativism	moral objectivism

a Arrange the following statements into statements that support moral relativism and statements that support moral objectivism.

i There is no such thing as right and wrong. It just depends on your own personal preference.

ii Moral values are not just personal opinions, they are permanent, always true, laws.

iii What we think is morally true are just social conventions based on our culture and upbringing.

iv Everyone's moral beliefs are just as valid as everybody else's.

v There are moral truths which are certain; they don't just depend on our own ego or desires.

vi By using our reason we can work out what is right and what is wrong.

b Do your own views come close to any of the views expressed in these statements? Explain your reasons.

The Catholic Church's view is that euthanasia is always wrong. However, not all Catholics agree with this view. Read the speech bubble to see what Hans Kung says. What do you think?

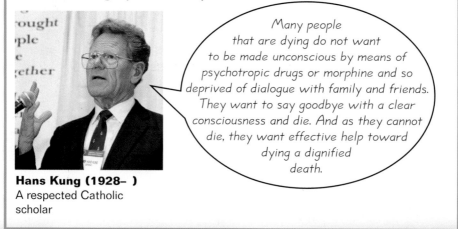

Hans Kung (1928–)
A respected Catholic scholar

Many people that are dying do not want to be made unconscious by means of psychotropic drugs or morphine and so deprived of dialogue with family and friends. They want to say goodbye with a clear consciousness and die. And as they cannot die, they want effective help toward dying a dignified death.

| 1 | 2 | 3 | 4 | 5 |

Euthanasia is sometimes justified

Euthanasia is always wrong

a Express your views about euthanasia on a scale of 1 to 5 and write your number on a piece of paper. Place all the papers into a box and shake them up. Have everyone take out one of the papers. Ask everyone with number 1 to form a line so as to make a human bar chart. Do the same for 2, 3, 4 and 5.

b Brainstorm reasons or ideas which support the view that euthanasia is always wrong and the view that euthanasia is sometimes justified. Arrange for half the class in groups to produce an argument in support of euthanasia while the other half in groups produce an argument against euthanasia.

Activity 7 Analyse the argument

With a partner choose argument (i) on infertility treatment or argument (ii) on gender roles, then analyse the argument carefully and answer these two questions.

a Is the argument based on a proposition?
If yes, is that proposition convincing?

b Is the argument persuasive or is it flawed in some way?

i Infertility treatment
Helping couples that are infertile to have a child using medical science is wrong. If a man or a woman cannot have a child for natural reasons, that is part of God's plan and God knows best. To try to get around what God has decided is to play at being God and that is wrong.

ii Gender roles
Both men and women have a role to play in family life. The natural role for men is to go out to work. However, for women, their natural role is to stay at home, do the shopping and look after the children. The roles of men and women are equally important but they are different.

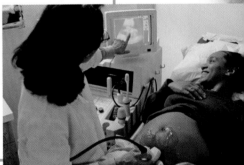

Activity 8 Find the flaw

Look at the four statements (a) to (d) then add two statements of your own that you think should be considered.

From the four statements (a) to (d), choose one that you think is flawed. Analyse the statement and explain why you think it is flawed.

a If God had intended us to fly, he would have given us wings.

b Cooking meat is against God's natural law and so is wrong.

c Cloning animals is unnatural and should be banned.

d Using artificial contraception to prevent pregnancy thwarts the will of God and so is wrong.

Moral duty theory

The neighbour from hell! I'm an expert on this subject. What's the story?

How would you solve a problem, Matt, with a noisy neighbour? Does the Golden Rule or natural law theory provide an answer?

The noisy neighbour

Jason is 19 years old and lives on his own. He enjoys playing a car-racing game on his games console. The lady who lives next door, Mrs Gorman, complains that the sound of screeching cars coming through the wall is very unpleasant and noisy. Using the Golden Rule, Jason might reason, 'I wouldn't like to be treated in the way I'm treating Mrs Gorman.' Or if he used the natural law theory, he might think, 'Being generally sociable is a natural human instinct.' Either way, he might decide to turn the volume down.

However, Jason in fact reasons, 'I really like the game with the volume turned up and anyway I don't care about Mrs Gorman's feelings and I don't care about any social instinct telling me to get on with people. I'm keeping the volume on full blast.'

Ah, the trusty old 'Am I bovvered?' argument. Not much you can do about that is there, Mrs G?

It is frustrating, I agree, Matt. How can you persuade someone who just doesn't care?

Activity 1 Changing Jason's mind

With a partner imagine you are a friend of Jason.

a How do you think Jason might be persuaded to change his mind?

b Put your advice on a Post-it note and display it to the rest of the class.

A rational basis to morals

For the Golden Rule or for natural law to influence how a person behaves, a great deal seems to depend on whether a person cares about other people. In some cases they have to care enough in order to stop doing something which they enjoy.

Towards the end of the eighteenth century, a professor of philosophy at Königsberg in Prussia published a number of books. These books very quickly had a major impact on how people thought about many subjects, including knowledge, truth, God, art and morals. His name was Immanuel Kant.

Immanuel Kant thought it must be possible to base morals on strong rational grounds.

Kant set out to discover one rational principle which would form the basis to all moral questions. In *Groundwork of the Metaphysics of Morals*, published in 1785, Kant laid out what he called 'the supreme principle of morality'. However, reading Kant is difficult. Even for people that are familiar with his ideas, Kant's writings are a real challenge.

Immanuel Kant (1724–1804)
'The present treatise is, however, nothing more than the investigation and establishment of the supreme principle of morality.'

Having a 'good will'

'The action was done neither from duty nor from direct inclination, but merely with a selfish view' (Immanuel Kant).

One idea that was important to Kant was 'good will'. Whether or not a person behaves in a moral way cannot be known by just looking at what they do. For a person's actions to be moral, the **motive** or purpose behind their actions must also be right. Their actions must be based on a 'good will'.

For example, if a shopkeeper always sells his goods at the correct price because he believes it his duty to be an honest shopkeeper, then he will be acting morally.

If a second shopkeeper sells his goods at the correct price only because he is worried that if he doesn't, his reputation will suffer and he will get fewer customers, then he will not be acting morally.

The first shopkeeper is honest because he believes in honesty for its own sake. Kant claims that this shopkeeper is behaving morally. The second shopkeeper's behaviour is a **means to an end**, as he doesn't want to lose any customers. Kant says that because he is motivated by personal advantage, he is not behaving morally.

Activity 2 What would Kant say?

In the story of the noisy neighbour, if Jason decided to turn down the volume on his games console, which of the following would Kant say showed him behaving morally? Explain your answer.

a Jason gets a letter from the local environment office that says it will take him to court if the noise continues.

b Jason's doctor tells him that he is showing early signs of hearing loss brought on by long-term exposure to loud sounds.

c Jason believes that it is his duty to avoid if possible being the source of pain or annoyance to another human being.

d Jason's girlfriend tells him that she will dump him if he doesn't spend less time on his games console.

'The hypothetical imperative only says that the action is good for some purpose' (Immanuel Kant).

A means to an end

The idea that to be moral a person's motive or purpose is important appears again when Kant writes about different kinds of motivation. A person may act because they want to achieve an end. For example, imagine Lewis wants a DJ mixing system. To raise the money, Lewis gets a job doing gardening work on a Saturday morning. Doing gardening work isn't something Lewis is motivated to do for its own sake. Gardening for Lewis isn't an end in itself, it is a means to an end. Kant called doing something as a means to an end a **hypothetical imperative**.

The categorical imperative

According to Kant, a different kind of motivation involves doing something for its own sake. A moral person doesn't do something because it will achieve an end. A moral person does something because they think it is the right thing to do. They believe it to be a moral duty. Kant called acting in this way a **categorical imperative**.

'The categorical imperative would be that which represented an action as necessary of itself without reference to another end' (Immanuel Kant).

Kant said that a true moral act has to be a categorical imperative. It is an act which one has to do not because of some other end. A moral act is an end in itself. You have to do it for its own sake because it is a moral duty.

With these ideas as a basis, Kant presents his moral duty theory.

Moral duty theory

A moral act is an act that a person has to do for its own sake. Because of this, one's own personal preferences – one's own likes or dislikes – do not come into it. A moral act has nothing to do with a person's personal preferences. A moral act is a moral duty which applies to everyone. An act that is morally true for one person would also be morally true for every person in that same situation.

Because of this, an act can be morally tested by asking, 'Can it be universalised and applied to everybody without this resulting in a contradiction?' If an act can pass this test, then it is a moral act.

Just as Isaac Newton had discovered a universal gravitational law, so Immanuel Kant believed he had discovered a universal moral law.

Whoa, where are my water wings? Did I suddenly fall in the deep end?

The idea of a moral duty that applies to everyone isn't as difficult as it sounds.

Universal moral duty

Kant deeply admired Isaac Newton. Newton had discovered a universal law of gravity which everything – stones, rocks, planets, water, apples – had to obey. In the same way, Kant believed he had discovered a universal law of morals which every human had to obey.

If I want the volume up full blast, I can.

According to Kant, the basis of this moral law was that any action could be shown to be moral by using a special test. If an action was universalised – if one imagined that it was a law which applied to everybody – would it work or would it lead to a contradiction? If it led to a contradiction, then the action could not be a moral one.

By having the volume turned up so loud that it irritates his neighbour, the noisy games player Jason is living part of his life by this rule: 'If I want something, even if that means irritating my neighbour, I can have it.'

33

What would happen if Jason turned his rule into a universal law? If Jason universalised his rule, it would be something like this: 'If anyone wants something, even if that means irritating their neighbour, they can have it.'

Jason would then very quickly see that his rule could never hold as a universal law. If Jason's universal law applied, everybody would be free to irritate each other. In a world where such a law applied, the law would contradict itself as very few people would get what they wanted. Using these ideas to solve moral problems is today often called **universalisation**.

How would it be if my rule were made into a universal law?

Hold it! Isn't universalising a rule the same as the Golden Rule – treat others as you would like them to treat you?

But if you universalise a rule, isn't that the same as saying, 'If everybody did this, you wouldn't like it, would you?'

Many have thought so. But Kant didn't think he had come up with a stuffy version of the Golden Rule.

But according to Kant, 'liking it' or 'not liking it' are irrelevant. He is asking, 'Can it be made into a universal law and if it can, does it contradict itself?'

Why all lying is wrong

Kant argued that all lying was wrong. He didn't claim that lying was wrong because people don't like being lied to. 'Liking' or 'not liking' depended on the whims of personal preference. For Kant, that was no basis for morals.

Nor did Kant claim that lying was wrong because people wouldn't trust you in the future, like the boy who cried wolf. If the villagers had never found out that the boy had lied, they would have continued to trust the boy, but that wouldn't make his lying moral. Kant claimed that the argument against lying was that lying involved a contradiction.

The boy who cried wolf is an example of consequence argument.

Kant on why lying is wrong

A person who lies hopes that their lie will be believed. This means that the universalised law which they will apply to everyone else is, 'Everyone will tell the truth'. Only in such a truth-telling world can they hope for their lies to be believed. But the rule which they will apply to themselves is, 'I will lie whenever it suits me'. However, they cannot turn this rule into a universalised law for everyone. For example, 'Everyone will lie whenever it suits them' would contradict the other rule they rely on, which is 'Everyone will tell the truth'.

Kant didn't use a consequence or outcome argument to claim that lying was wrong.

Testing the principle

Kant knew perfectly well that reason alone wouldn't make people behave in a moral way. He understood that often the heart, not the head ruled human behaviour. Kant wouldn't have claimed that his moral duty theory would suddenly change a self-centred, noisy neighbour like Jason into a considerate and warm-hearted human being. To be a moral person, Kant believed, a great deal depended on how that person was brought up and the examples they learnt when young from the people around them. However, Kant also believed that humans are rational beings that respond to reason.

Kant's ethical theory soon came in for a good deal of criticism. In 1787 the Swiss philosopher Benjamin Constant suggested that Kant's theory, when put to the test with specific cases, came up with some very doubtful moral judgements. Perhaps the clearest example is what has become known as the **benevolent lie**.

Benjamin Constant (1767–1830)
'No man has a right to a truth that injures others.'

The benevolent lie

According to Kant's theory, always telling the truth was a moral duty. But Benjamin Constant said that lying in certain specific cases was morally the right thing to do. Benjamin Constant argues that a benevolent lie is justified. A benevolent lie is when a person is dishonest because it will bring more good than evil or because it will help avoid a terrible evil.

The benevolent lie

Imagine that a known murderer wants to kill a girl called Anne. You know Anne is hiding in an attic in a building nearby. The murderer demands that you tell him where Anne is hiding.
Does it make any sense in this situation to say that you have a moral duty to tell the truth? Even saying 'I have nothing to say' or 'I know but I will not tell you' could place Anne in extreme danger as your shifty answer might cause the murderer to suspect that Anne is close by.
If you tell the murderer where Anne is, the likely outcome is that she will be murdered. In such a situation isn't lying the moral thing to do? Telling the truth isn't always a moral duty. Lying in order to save the life of an innocent person would be justified.

Anne Frank (1929–1944)
She was 13 when she hid from the Nazis. After two years, Anne and her family were betrayed and arrested by the German security police. Seven months later she died of typhus in a concentration camp.

Activity 3 Is a benevolent lie justified?

Imagine in 1942 you are approached by a Nazi officer. He questions you about where Anne Frank and her family are. You know the family are hiding in a nearby house. Is it your moral duty to tell the truth, or do you have a moral duty to lie? Explain your answer.

A duty to speak the truth

'To be truthful in all declarations is therefore a sacred unconditional command of reason, and not limited by any expediency' (Immanuel Kant).

In his essay 'On a Supposed Right to Tell Lies from Benevolent Motives', Kant defended his ideas from Benjamin Constant's criticism. Kant claimed that nobody had a right to lie in any circumstances. If we have to speak, we must always be honest, even though it may cause us great difficulties or bring suffering to someone else.

Kant insisted that a moral judgement cannot be based on a consequence or an outcome which may or may not come about. Kant believed that basing moral judgements on possible consequences was unpredictable and could result in an even worse outcome.

For example, if a known murderer asks where Anne is, you may think you are helping her by sending the murderer off in the wrong direction. However, unknown to you, Anne has left her hiding place and accidentally bumps into the murderer. Because you lied, Anne is arrested and loses her life.

Had you told the truth, the murderer would have gone to the hiding place, found Anne missing and perhaps decided to give up. You would have told the truth and Anne would have survived.

Activity 4 Is a benevolent lie justified?

A husband is trapped in his car after a road accident. It is likely that he will die. His wife has already been removed from the wreckage but she is dead. The husband asks the doctor, 'How's my wife?' Do you think the doctor should tell him the truth or a lie? Explain your answer.

A white lie

A white lie is not the same as a benevolent lie. A benevolent lie is motivated by a good cause like achieving a greater good or helping to avoid an evil.

A **white lie** may also be motivated by a good cause but a white lie is never about anything really important. Often a white lie is used to flatter, be polite or be tactful with people.

A white lie is often used to flatter, be polite or be tactful with people.

For example, your mum buys herself a new hat which she loves. When she gets home she puts it on and says, 'What do you think?' You may think the hat looks terrible but to avoid hurting her feelings you say, 'It looks great, mum.'

Kant believed that white lies were trivial. From a moral point of view, telling a white lie didn't matter one way or the other.

But if I've got this right, God doesn't come into Kant's moral theory at all. This isn't a religious ethic.

And also animals, Matt. Kant didn't believe universal laws applied to animals. But let's look at Kant and religion.

A religious ethic?

Immanuel Kant was a deeply religious man.

Kant was a deeply religious man. He was brought up as a Christian and strong Christian ideas can be seen in his writing. He certainly believed in God. Indeed he believed that on moral grounds it is necessary to assume the existence of God. However, by claiming a rational basis to morals, he is very clearly declaring that you can have morals without God.

Kant's argument also claims that if you are not religious, that doesn't mean you can do what you like because there are no rules. The world isn't like a playground with no playground attendant telling you what to do. Every human being has a responsibility to behave morally, whether or not they believe in God.

Three big ideas

Many of Kant's ideas are used in moral discussions today. Three big ideas that stand out are motive, means to an end and universalisation.

Motive

Morality is about your motive or purpose. If you are about to steal from a shop but decide that you shouldn't, that might look like a moral act. But if you only do so because you spot a surveillance camera, then it is self-interest and not moral goodness that is governing your behaviour.

Is he motivated by self-interest?

Means to an end

No one should be used as a mere thing or as a way of getting to some other goal. Kant's ideas give status to the individual and have been used to defend the rights of the individual.

Universalisation

Suppose everybody acted in that way? Asking questions like this continues to form the basis of many moral arguments today. Central to the principle of universalisation are questions like these: How would it be if everyone behaved in this way? If this is right for you, is it also right for everyone else?

Kant's ideas have been used to defend the rights of the individual.

Some of the key things to learn:

Moral duty theory

- Moral duty theory is an attempt to discover a moral principle based on reason and which doesn't depend on whether a person happens to care, or on their likes or dislikes.

- The theory claims that a moral action cannot be one motivated by self-interest. A moral action must be based on 'good will'.

- The theory also claims that a true moral act is not a means to an end. It is a moral duty undertaken for its own sake.

Immanuel Kant (1724–1804)

> How would it be if my rule were made into a universal law?

Universalisation

- Universalisation is based on the claim that what is morally true for one person must also be true for every person in that same situation.

- Universalisation can be put simply in the form of a question: How would it be if my rule were made into a law which everybody had to obey?

- If such a rule can't be turned into a law for everybody without creating a contradiction, it will not be morally right to follow that rule.

The benevolent lie

- Immanuel Kant claimed that telling the truth was always a moral duty.

- The benevolent lie is based on the claim that sometimes lying is the right thing to do, such as not telling a known murderer where his intended victim is hiding.

- One objection to the benevolent lie is that consequences are unpredictable and the good you hope to achieve by lying may go badly wrong.

Unit 4 Things to do

With a partner consider the following examples. Are some of the examples **benevolent lies** and therefore justified in the circumstances? Are some **white lies** that have no moral importance? Are all of them simply lies and so cannot be justified? Explain your answer.

a While kicking a ball around in the garden you break a window. When your dad asks, 'Do you know how the window got broken?' You reply, 'I don't know anything about it, Dad.'

b For Christmas you are hoping to get a book on astronomy but instead your aunty gives you a book on astrology. When you take off the wrapping you say, 'That's great, Aunty. It looks really interesting. Thank you.'

c Your older brother Kevin takes the day off work because he wants to watch the international football match live on TV at 3.00 p.m. He gets his girlfriend to phone his boss. On the phone she says, 'Kevin has a bad stomach and won't be able to come to work today.'

d After looking at the X-rays, a doctor realises that his elderly patient has only about three months to live. The patient asks, 'How long have I got, Doctor?' The doctor replies, 'I don't want you to worry. If you look after yourself, you've still got quite a few more years in you yet.'

e During an enemy attack, a young soldier runs away but in his panic he runs into a minefield and dies. His commander writes to the young soldier's parents, 'He was a good soldier who died honourably in the service of his country.'

f You are organising a surprise birthday party for Jack, your boyfriend. While sorting out the arrangements you talk to one of Jack's friends. Jack sees you and asks, 'What were you talking about?' You reply, 'Oh, nothing much, it was just about a TV programme.'

Universalising an issue, or asking how it would be if everybody behaved that way, is often used to decide whether an action is moral or not.

a Choose one of the following statements. Now ask, 'How would it be if the rule were made into a universal law for everybody?' What answer do you get? Explain your thinking.

i People dying of hunger in countries far away isn't something we have to do anything about.	**ii** If a person is offensive about your religion, then using violence is justified.	**iii** If a boss decides not to give a person a job because of the colour of their skin, that is their decision and has nothing to do with anyone else.

39

b Do you think that universalising an issue helps when deciding if something is right or wrong? Does universalising an issue have any strengths or weaknesses? Explain your answer.

Activity 7 Pyramid

Liam steals money, watches, mobile phones, etc., from the bags and jackets left in the changing rooms. Which of the triangles best completes the sentence 'Liam shouldn't steal because …'?

Arrange the six triangles into a pyramid. At the top of the pyramid, put the reason you agree with the most. Put your second and third choices underneath. At the base of the pyramid, put the three reasons you agree with the least. If you do not really agree with any of these reasons, write a triangle of your own. Explain your answer.

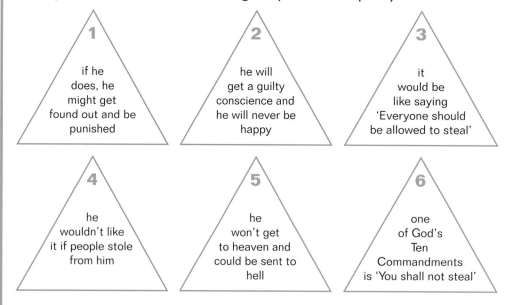

1 if he does, he might get found out and be punished

2 he will get a guilty conscience and he will never be happy

3 it would be like saying 'Everyone should be allowed to steal'

4 he wouldn't like it if people stole from him

5 he won't get to heaven and could be sent to hell

6 one of God's Ten Commandments is 'You shall not steal'

Activity 8 Agree or disagree?

Choose one of the following statements. Do you agree or disagree with the statement? Explain your answer.

a If a person doesn't learn when young to care about other people, they will never find real happiness when they are an adult.

b Without the fear that God is watching us, like a giant surveillance camera in the sky, moral standards will decline.

c To be a moral person you have to be religious.

d You can have anything you want and you can do anything to get it. This is the rule to live by today.

Unit 5
Utilitarianism

In eighteenth-century Europe, during a period now known as the **Enlightenment**, there was a widespread willingness to discuss new ideas. Many traditional beliefs about religion, morals and how people should be ruled were questioned.

An idea that was talked about a lot at this time was the claim that morality wasn't about obeying a natural law or about God's commandments. Instead, Claude Helvetius (1715–1771) in France and Cesare Beccaria (1738–1794) in Italy argued that morality was about increasing happiness.

In England, the chemist and Christian minister Joseph Priestley (1733–1804) had very similar views. However, the person in England that did most to develop a moral theory based on happiness was a lawyer called Jeremy Bentham.

Artists, philosophers and writers met in the evening to discuss new ideas about religion, morality and government. They called their meetings soirées from the French word *soir* 'evening'.

At first, Bentham explained his ideas using the phrase 'the greatest happiness of the greatest number'. Other thinkers had also used these words. Bentham continued to admire the phrase but in his book *An Introduction to the Principles of Morals and Legislation*, published in 1789, he suggested an improved version. This time his morality was based on what he called the **Principle of Utility**. 'Utility' means 'something which is useful' in the sense of bringing about more happiness and Bentham's way of thinking was called **utilitarianism**. Today, Jeremy Bentham's Principle of Utility is usually called the **happiness principle**.

Jeremy Bentham (1748–1832)

'It is the greatest happiness of the greatest number that is the measure of right and wrong.'

The happiness principle

Whether something is right or wrong depends on how much it will increase happiness or increase suffering. The more happiness an action causes, the more good it is. The more suffering an action causes, the more wrong it is.

To weigh up how much happiness an action causes, certain things have to be taken into account. For example, if an action leads to long-lasting happiness, then that counts for more than just short-term happiness. Intense happiness counts for more than just mild happiness. The high likelihood of happiness counts for more than just the possibility of happiness. The happiness of a lot of people counts for more than the happiness of just a few people.

Strewth! Have you got a calculator? Makes morals sound like doing arithmetic. Have you got an example, Mrs G, to show what Bentham was on about?

Try this one about Mrs Hughes' drive.

Mrs Hughes' Drive

Every school day Mrs Hughes drives her three small children to the local primary school and then goes to work as a senior nurse in a large hospital. For the past week, her front drive has been blocked by a truck which belongs to a builder who is working on the house next door. Sometimes with difficulty Mrs Hughes has been able to manoeuvre out of her drive and around the truck but other times she has found it impossible. The children have been late for school and Mrs Hughes has been late for work.

Mrs Hughes has asked the builder not to block her drive. The builder has said that he has got to unload his materials and he can't be expected to park further down the road and carry materials and tools up to the house. 'Anyway,' he says, 'what's your problem? You can easily get around my truck. I could drive a bus through that gap!' The job is expected to take the builder a month to complete.

Is Mrs Hughes wrong to complain? Is the builder right to park his truck outside Mrs Hughes' house?

Activity 1 Mrs Hughes' drive

Explain whether Mrs Hughes or the builder has right on their side, expressing your own personal view. Use Jeremy Bentham's happiness principle in your explanation. Try to make your argument convincing.

Utilitarianism and suffering

For Bentham, it was clearly wrong if a person had to suffer pain or have their happiness reduced. If a lot of people had to suffer a lot of pain, that was even more wrong.

Bentham didn't believe that he had to prove that suffering was wrong. For him, such a claim was self-evident. He argued that it was a basic proposition. It was the start of the proof for his moral theory and a proof had to start somewhere.

However, perhaps for many people at the time, what was so surprising about Bentham's thinking was his claim that all suffering was wrong, no matter who suffered it. If a husband made his wife miserable, treating her as a domestic servant, that was wrong. If a factory owner allowed conditions in his factory

'Women, whether married or not, have been placed in a state of perpetual wardship' (Jeremy Bentham).

to be dangerous, that was also wrong. Bentham said that one person's happiness was to count as equal to another person's happiness, regardless of sex, rank, class, colour or nationality. This could be summed up in one memorable phrase attributed to Bentham: 'Everybody to count for one, nobody for more than one.'

Utilitarianism and social reform

Jeremy Bentham was a social reformer; that is, he wanted to see a change in many of the laws in Britain because he believed that a large number of laws were unjust and immoral. Bentham and his followers believed that, using utilitarianism, they could show that these laws were wrong.

'As soon as slavery is established, it becomes the lot of the greatest number. ... The advantage is only on the side of a single person; the disadvantages are on the side of the multitude'
(Jeremy Bentham).

For example, at that time many people in Britain had made huge sums of money legally through slavery. Bentham argued that although slavery might make a slave owner wealthy and happy, that happiness was far outweighed by the intense misery suffered by the hundreds, perhaps thousands of slaves he owned.

Animal suffering

Although many Christians had shown compassion and kindness towards animals, the main tradition of the Christian faith for over a thousand years was that the treatment of animals was not a moral issue.

The Bible says, 'Let mankind have dominion over the fish of the sea, and over the birds of the air, and over the cattle, and over all the earth, and over every creeping thing' (Genesis Ch 1 v 26). The word 'dominion' was interpreted as meaning 'domination' over all animals. Thomas Aquinas, who was regarded as one of the great masters of moral and religious doctrine, seemed to have confirmed this view by writing, 'It matters not how man behaves to animals, because God has subjected all things to man's power. ... God does not ask of man what he does with oxen or other animals.'

'The day may come when the rest of the animal creation may acquire those rights. ... The question is not, Can they reason?, nor Can they talk? but, Can they suffer?'
(Jeremy Bentham).

Utilitarianism, however, claimed that as animals could suffer, being the cause of animal suffering was a moral issue. Blood sports like bear-baiting were increasingly viewed as being wrong. Bear-baiting involved chaining a bear and getting dogs to attack it while spectators gambled on whether the dogs or the bear would win.

Using utilitarianism, it was argued that although the spectators might get some pleasure out of the spectacle, this was nothing compared with the suffering endured by the bear and the dogs. Bear-baiting was banned in Britain in 1835.

Activity 2 Fox-hunting ban

a Fox-hunting was banned in England and Wales in 2004. On a scale of 1 to 5, do you think it was right or wrong to ban fox-hunting?

1	2	3	4	5

It is wrong to have banned fox-hunting

It is right to have banned fox-hunting

b Explain your answer. Use utilitarianism to support your view or to give a view which differs from your own.

Flaws or weaknesses

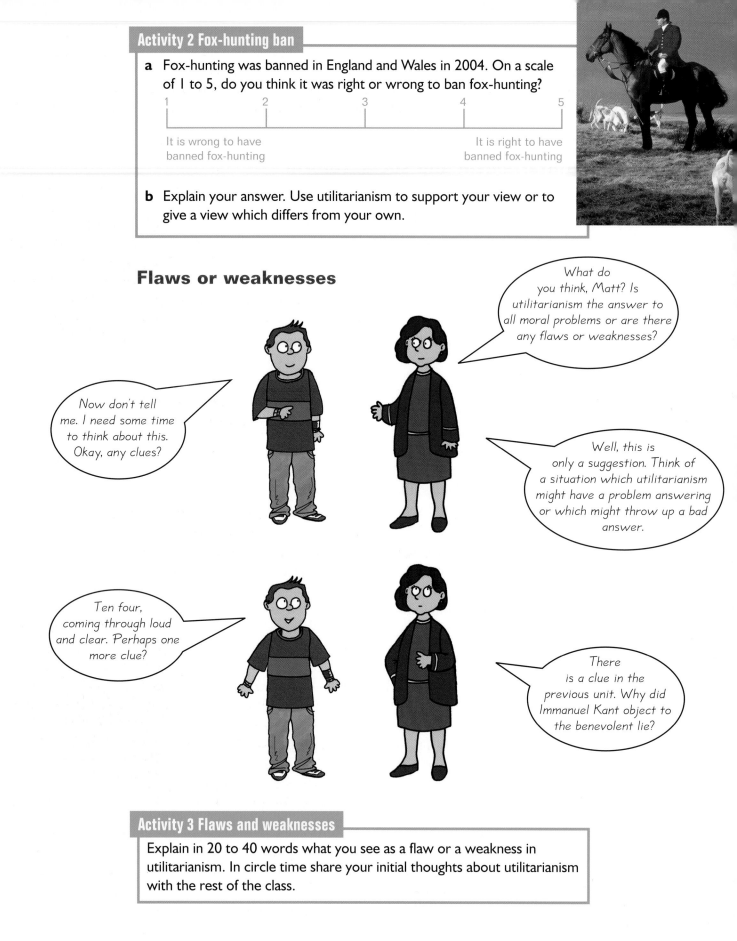

What do you think, Matt? Is utilitarianism the answer to all moral problems or are there any flaws or weaknesses?

Now don't tell me. I need some time to think about this. Okay, any clues?

Well, this is only a suggestion. Think of a situation which utilitarianism might have a problem answering or which might throw up a bad answer.

Ten four, coming through loud and clear. Perhaps one more clue?

There is a clue in the previous unit. Why did Immanuel Kant object to the benevolent lie?

Activity 3 Flaws and weaknesses

Explain in 20 to 40 words what you see as a flaw or a weakness in utilitarianism. In circle time share your initial thoughts about utilitarianism with the rest of the class.

Public and private problems

One criticism levelled at utilitarianism is that it often seems to give clearer answers to public issues – issues that affect a lot of people. When the suffering of a large number of slaves is compared with the happiness of a small number of slave owners, it seems clear that the misery of the slaves vastly outweighs the advantages enjoyed by the slave owners.

But when it comes to private problems that involve small numbers of people like friends, neighbours, brothers and sisters, utilitarianism doesn't always appear to be able to provide a clear answer. Who's to say a sister's high level of enjoyment from watching a thought-provoking TV programme about the human genome is outweighed by the enjoyment of her two brothers from watching a live football match on a different channel?

Who's to say a sister's wish to watch a TV programme is outweighed by the wish of her two brothers?

Jeremy Bentham was certainly much more interested in public law and how it affected large numbers of people rather than private issues which involved only small numbers of people.

Predicting consequences

In the eighteenth century, Joseph Butler was a minister in the Church of England. He went on to become Bishop of Durham. His work *Fifteen Sermons on Human Nature* was published in 1726. Although written some 50 years before Jeremy Bentham's ideas, these sermons by Joseph Butler presented a challenge to utilitarian thinking.

Not competent judges

Experience teaches us that in many cases we are not very competent to judge whether an action will result in good or harm. Very often we may be led astray by our own passions or private interest. The real outcome or consequences of our actions are difficult to predict. This lack of certainty should teach us to be cautious.

Where we see obvious signs of suffering, perhaps in a person who is close to us or whose circumstances we know, we do have a real chance of doing something that will reduce their suffering.

However, trying to promote positive happiness is much more difficult. Therefore it is better to put effort into reducing suffering rather than to trust in our uncertain ability to increase happiness.

Joseph Butler (1692–1752)
'We are not competent judges, whether a particular action will upon the whole do good or harm.'

In a group of three or four, make up and present a short play about a
character or characters that try to increase happiness but find that things
go very wrong due to unforeseen circumstances or the difficulty of
predicting consequences.

A godless doctrine?

In spite of these criticisms, many people with and without a religious
faith continue to make moral judgements based on utilitarian ideas.
For example, in Pope Paul VI's famous 1968 letter *Humanae Vitae*
'On Human Life', one of the arguments put forward is that the use
of artificial contraception can result in a man treating a woman as 'a
mere instrument of selfish enjoyment'. Artificial contraception, it is
claimed, can destroy the happiness and companionship that a man
and a woman living together can enjoy. It can result in men treating
women as merely objects to be used. That artificial contraception can
damage the relationship between women and men and so increases
unhappiness between partners, it is claimed, is an argument based on
utilitarian principles.

Although utilitarian arguments may be used by people with a
religious faith, is utilitarianism a religious ethic? John Stuart Mill
was one of the leading supporters of utilitarianism in the nineteenth
century. Jeremy Bentham was John Stuart Mill's godfather and had
a deep influence on Mill's thinking. John Stuart Mill argued that
utilitarianism wasn't a 'godless doctrine'. His argument may be
expressed as follows.

John Stuart Mill (1806–1873)
'Utility is not only not a godless doctrine,
but more profoundly religious than any
other.'

Is utilitarianism a 'godless doctrine'?

Utilitarianism is not a 'godless doctrine'. It would be
very odd to conceive of God as a being that would create
the universe in order to then watch humans and animals
suffer. What does that say about the moral character of
God?

If it is a true belief that God's will, above all things, is
the happiness of his creatures and that this was God's
purpose in creating them, then utilitarianism is not a
'godless doctrine'. As utilitarianism also seeks to increase
happiness everywhere, God and utilitarianism seek the
same thing. It follows from this that utilitarianism is not
a 'godless doctrine' but is more profoundly religious than
any other.

The happiness principle

- Doing something that increases happiness is a good thing. Doing something that increases suffering is a bad thing.

- The happiness of a lot of people usually counts for more than the happiness of a few.

- As well as numbers of people made happy, when deciding on what is right or wrong, other things have to be considered such as the intensity, duration and certainty of the happiness.

Jeremy Bentham (1748–1832)

Flaws and weaknesses

- Utilitarianism seems to provide clearer answers in public matters which involve large numbers of people.

- Answers are less clear when utilitarianism is used for private or domestic problems which involve small numbers of people such as neighbours, friends and family.

- Utilitarianism requires the need to predict future consequences and this always lacks certainty.

Is a sister's wish to watch a TV programme outweighed by the wish of her two brothers?

A godless doctrine?

- It would be very odd to conceive of God as a being that would create the universe in order to then watch humans or animals suffer.

- If it is true that God's will is the happiness of his creatures, then this goal of happiness is the same goal sought by utilitarianism.

- As the will of God and the goal of utilitarianism are the same, utilitarianism is not a 'godless doctrine', but is more profoundly religious than any other doctrine.

John Stuart Mill (1806–1873)

Unit 5 Things to do

a Organise a class debate on the following motion:

This house believes that using rats for medical research is wrong and should be banned.

Arrange two teams of four, one team to speak for the motion and one team to speak against. Agree a time limit for speakers of 1–2 minutes. Ensure contributions to the debate may be made from all other members of the class.

Arrange for three reporters to identify and record any use of utilitarian arguments, natural law arguments or divine command arguments.

b Following the debate, arrange for a class vote. This may take the form of a secret ballot using voting slips with this wording:

Motion: This house believes that using rats for medical research is wrong and should be banned.

Tick one of the boxes to express your view:

I am for the motion ☐
I am against the motion ☐
I abstain ☐

Activity 6 Who do you save?

Your younger brother Collin is aged 12. He is often reckless and has frequently been in trouble at school and with the police. His teachers say he won't amount to much. Josh, who has only just arrived in the neighbourhood, is the same age as Collin. Josh is highly intelligent. His science teacher regards him as one of the most promising students he has ever taught. Josh is interested in the causes of disease. He hopes one day to become a doctor and to do medical research.

One day Collin and Josh are in a boat on a river. You warn them both to be careful because the current is strong. But Collin stands up in the boat and larks about. The boat tilts over and both boys fall into the water. Both boys are dragged under by the current and are drowning. You dive into the river and swim towards the boys but you know you will only be able to save one first and the other is likely to drown.

a Do you have a moral duty to save your brother Collin first or to save Josh? What do you decide to do? Explain your reasoning.

b Does utilitarianism help to give an answer in situations like this or does it show that utilitarianism doesn't really work in some cases?

Activity 7 Persuasive or flawed?

Here are five arguments that use utilitarian principles. Choose one. Is the argument persuasive or is it in some way flawed? Explain your answer.

1. Oxfam donation

A sum of £30 given to Oxfam to relieve poverty in a developing country would buy a lot more happiness than £30 spent on an MP3 player with a bigger memory to give to an 11 year old girl in a developed country who already has a lot of clothes, toys and electrical gadgets.

A sum of £30 could buy a lot of happiness for an 11 year old girl in a developing country.

2. Mother's dilemma

The loss of life suffered by an aborted foetus would be a lot less than the suffering a mother and her family of three on social security would experience if that mother had to feed, clothe and look after a fourth child.

3. Wild tigers

The freedom and happiness a tiger gets from living in the wild is worth much more than any happiness visitors get from looking at that tiger in a zoo.

4. Out-of-work father

A desperate out-of-work father steals an iPod from a department store so that his son can have something for his birthday. The father gives his son a lot of happiness which outweighs the loss to the department store, a loss so small that the store will hardly notice.

5. Terror accomplice

An accomplice knows where a terrorist has planted a bomb. A security officer suggests using use force to get the information. The officer says, 'What the accomplice will suffer will be small compared to what hundreds will suffer if we don't get the information.'

Activity 8 Uncle Jim's dilemma

Uncle Jim has no children of his own. When Christmas arrives, Uncle Jim has saved up £120 which he plans to give to his two nieces and his nephew. Jim's well-off sister has two girls called Collette and Amy. Jim's brother has little money and a boy called Tom. Uncle Jim could divide up the money and give the three children £40 each to spend on whatever they fancy.

However, Collette and Amy seem to have everything they want. Tom never seems to get much for Christmas. Tom gets to play a school clarinet but he says he would love to have a clarinet of his own so he could practise more at home. Two days before Christmas, Uncle Jim walks past a music shop and sees a clarinet on sale in the window. The price is £110.

a   What do you think Uncle Jim should do? Explain your answer.

b   Does the happiness principle help to resolve Jim's dilemma?

c   Are other moral theories more helpful? Consider theories like divine command theory, the Golden Rule and natural law.

Unit 6
Situation ethics

According to John's Gospel, Jesus gave some final instructions to his disciples on their last night together. Jesus said to his disciples, 'And now I give you a new commandment: love one another. As I have loved you, so you must love one another' (John Ch 13 v 34). These words have come to be known as the **Law of Love**.

'And now I give you a new commandment: Love one another' (Jesus of Nazareth).

Jesus and the law

Jesus had often talked about love before; for example, 'Love your neighbour' (Mark Ch 12 v 28–31), 'Love your enemies' (Matthew Ch 5 v 43). However, on this occasion, Jesus puts his teaching in the form of a law. This was unusual. Jesus rarely put his teaching in the form of a law.

One method that Jesus used a lot was to teach people through stories, or parables, such as the Good Samaritan, the Prodigal Son, the Good Shepherd, the Sheep and the Goats. All of these stories have a moral message but Jesus doesn't state the message of the story in the form of a law.

Sidelining the law

Jesus also made his moral views known in the way he treated people and in what he actually did. Unlike earlier Jewish teachers such as Moses, the impression some people get is that Jesus wasn't that interested in fixed laws. In fact, Jesus seems to have been prepared to sideline or even break the ancient law given to Moses. For people brought up in Judaism, however, these were no ordinary laws. They were commandments that had come from God. They had been given to Moses at Mount Sinai and had been passed down and taught for over a thousand years.

The man with a paralysed hand (Mark Ch 3 v 1–6)

The woman caught in adultery (John Ch 8 v 3–11)

50

Activity 1 Jesus and the law

Look at the pictures of the woman caught in adultery and the man with a paralysed hand, two occasions when Jesus seems to have sidelined or even broken the law. Choose one picture.

a Explain the Bible story which goes with this picture.

b Explain in what way, if at all, the story shows Jesus sidelining or even breaking the ancient law of Moses.

Fulfilling the law

The usual way in which Christians have interpreted Jesus' attitude to the law of Moses was to say that Jesus had 'fulfilled the law'. Jesus, it was said, hadn't thrown out the idea that there were certain God-given commandments – not killing, not stealing, not lying, not committing adultery, etc. – which were universally valid laws, true for all time. Jesus had deepened and fulfilled these commandments.

However, in the twentieth century, Christian thinkers like Emil Brunner and Dietrich Bonhoeffer questioned this interpretation. Bonhoeffer, in particular, pointed out that Jesus simply didn't seem to be interested in a 'universally valid proposition or a law'.

But the person that most clearly made the claim that Jesus' ethics were not about a set of permanent laws was Joseph Fletcher, an American professor of Christian ethics and Episcopalian priest. He published his **controversial** ideas in a book called *Situation Ethics*, which came out in 1966.

'The situation ethic … is an ethic of making decisions rather than "looking them up" in a manual of prefab rules.'
Joseph Fletcher (1905–1991)

Situation ethics

The belief that answers to moral problems can be found by looking them up in a manual of rules does not work. Rules such as 'do not steal' and 'do not lie' give the right moral answers in most situations. However, human life is so complex and varied that it is wrong to blindly follow the rules and always to treat them as absolute and rigid rules which must never be broken.

Jesus was telling us to look at each situation for ourselves and to figure out the best choice for that situation. The best choice is the most loving choice. To solve a moral issue, we should ask ourselves this question: 'What is the most loving thing possible in this situation?' The answer to that question is the right moral response in that situation.

> Jesus breaking the rules! Seriously, was Jesus really that controversial?

> It's an interpretation of Jesus' life, but there is evidence to support it. Joseph Fletcher and many other scholars believed Jesus was against legalism – rigid rules which brought pain and suffering to life.

Glittering generality

Is abortion wrong? Is adultery wrong? Is sex outside marriage wrong? Is war wrong? Joseph Fletcher recognises that all these look like questions to which we should be able to give a clear answer. However, the fact is that humans disagree.

For Joseph Fletcher, the problem is not to do with our ability to make moral judgements. The problem is with the nature of the questions. He calls a question like 'Is abortion wrong?' a glittering generality. It is a question about abortion in general.

Joseph Fletcher says that to make a moral judgement about abortion in general will result in harsh decisions which bring pain and suffering to people's lives. To answer a moral question correctly, it is necessary to look at one case, one situation on its own, and make a judgement about that one situation. This means that abortion may be right in some situations but wrong in other situations. According to **situation ethics**, moral judgements can only be made about a specific situation. A moral judgement can't be generalised and turned into an absolute rule that works in all situations.

Is war wrong? Is euthanasia wrong? Situation ethics says that to answer such questions you need a specific case, a real situation.

Abortion – a specific situation

A rape victim is made pregnant. What is the most loving thing possible in this situation?

To make his point, Joseph Fletcher describes many specific situations. One of the most famous situations he describes is the case of a rape victim.

In 1962 an unmarried girl suffering from a severe mental illness is a patient in a hospital. In the hospital she is attacked, raped and made pregnant by a violent and disturbed patient. Due to the severity of their mental illness, neither the girl nor her attacker are able to bring up a child. The girl's father complains, claiming that the hospital had failed to protect his daughter. He asks that his daughter should be allowed an abortion. The staff and administrators of the hospital refuse the father's request on the grounds that the existing law only allows the girl to have an abortion if her life is in danger.

After describing the details of the case, Joseph Fletcher asks this question: 'Is not the most loving thing possible (the right thing) in this case to terminate the pregnancy?'

Activity 2 Fletcher's abortion example

a In groups of two or three, discuss the case of the mentally ill girl who was raped. What do you think is the right thing to do in this situation? Explain your point of view.

b Survey the views of different faith communities. What view do they take of the rape case Joseph Fletcher describes? Do they agree or disagree with Joseph Fletcher that the right thing to do in this case is to abort the pregnancy?

A licence for permissiveness

Edwin Williams was the principal at the Bible College in Melbourne, Australia. In 1972 he published 'Situation Ethics: The New Morality', a short article where he argued that although situation ethics had certain strengths, it also had several weaknesses. One of these was that 'love' could become a justification for doing whatever you want. It was a licence that permitted anything.

Edwin Williams (1906–1994)
'Love left to itself … can easily turn into the licence of permissiveness.'

The 'love is ambiguous' argument

The suggestion that we can solve moral problems by acting in the most loving way possible may sound straightforward but, in fact, 'love' doesn't tell us very clearly what we ought to do. 'Love' is **ambiguous** and is open to **subjective** interpretation. If 'love' is used as the basis for making moral judgements, it can easily turn into every person doing what they think is right in their own eyes. It is a licence for **permissiveness**. In view of the difficulty of knowing exactly what is the loving thing to do in any given situation, the guidance of the Church and long-established values should be taken seriously and not easily set aside.

Is acting in 'the most loving way possible' too ambiguous to be useful? If we judge a situation on the basis of 'the most loving thing we can do', is that simply a way to justify doing whatever we want? In order to think about that question, consider Sadie's choice.

Sadie's choice

What is the right thing that Sadie should do?

Sadie and Simon are both aged 15. Sadie has been going out with Simon for the past two months. She likes Simon a lot. She feels he is safe and she knows she can trust him. Recently, however, Rory, who is 16, has shown Sadie a lot of interest. Rory is very confident, he makes Sadie laugh a lot and he is very popular with the other girls. She suspects that having Rory as a boyfriend would be a lot more fun than Simon. One day, while hanging around in a school corridor, Rory tells Sadie that on Saturday afternoon a band he plays in are performing at a local club. He gives her a ticket to the gig and asks her to come along, 'Afterwards, we can go for a pizza.' Sadie says, 'You know I can't, Rory. I'm already seeing Simon.' Rory says, 'So what? I'm not going to tell him. Come out with me on Saturday. You'll enjoy yourself and Simon will never know.'

a In groups of two or three, come up with at least three different options open to Sadie.

b Discuss in groups the three options identified and decide what would be the right thing for Sadie to do. Explain your answer.

c Do you think situation ethics gives Sadie a licence to do anything she wants?

Agape or unconditional love

Defenders of situation ethics argue that 'love' isn't as ambiguous as its critics have claimed. Joseph Fletcher argued that what he had meant by 'love' wasn't some sort of permissive, hippie, anything-goes love. He had meant the sort of love Jesus had taught and shown in his own life, and that was Christian love or **agape**.

An example of agape is the unconditional love a good father or mother may show for their child.

The writers of the New Testament chose 'agape', a rarely used Greek word, to get across Jesus' meaning when he talked about love. Agape involved kindness and help towards others which was freely given and did not expect anything back in return. It was love given without any conditions, or unconditional love. A person showed agape if they were prepared to put themselves out or if they made a sacrifice for the sake of another person. An example of agape is the unconditional love a good father or mother may give to their own child.

The Greeks viewed agape as very different from **eros**. Eros meant the sort of romantic, passionate, erotic love that existed between a man and a woman. When Jesus said, 'Love your enemies', he didn't have erotic love in mind.

Agape was also different from **philia**, another Greek word for a type of love. Philia involved mutual advantage such as between two friends who both gain something from their friendship. One friend helps the other but knows that the other friend will help them when they need it. Philia wasn't a one-sided sacrifice. Philia was conditional love and the condition was: I'll help you, but when I need help, you'll help me.

Selective quoting

Many Christians today, even if they have not heard of Joseph Fletcher, would agree with his claim that it is suspect to use the Bible to find a quotation or a rule which seems to give an answer to a moral problem. It could easily result in people quoting those parts of the Bible which provided the answer they wanted to hear. This would be a form of selective quoting. At its worst, selective quoting is a dishonest attempt to mislead. The intention is to take a quotation or several quotations from the Bible and to claim this is what the Bible says. A more honest study of the Bible may reveal a very different message that has a stronger claim to be the Bible's message. This might be because the second message reflects the Bible as a whole, or because it reflects parts of the Bible that have a higher claim to authority.

An example of moral life

Although they do not accept Joseph Fletcher's wiliness to abandon all rules other than the Law of Love, many Christians believe that agape is central to the way they should try to live a moral life. Agape, they believe, is seen in the qualities that Jesus showed, qualities like kindness, mercy, honesty, forgiveness, avoidance of violence, and self-sacrifice. Agape often shows itself in a willingness to help people even if they are not very likeable or even if they have done you wrong.

Left: Jesus and Zacchaeus the tax collector (Luke Ch 19 v 1–10).

Right: Jesus and the servant of the high priest (Matthew Ch 26 v 51–52).

Activity 4 Examples of agape?

Look at the pictures which show two events in Jesus' life. Choose one of these events and find out the details of what happened.

a What qualities in Jesus do you think this event shows? Explain your answer.

b Describe an example, real or fictional, of a person showing agape.

God revealed in Jesus

Many Christians believe that Jesus provides a perfect example of what a moral life should be. As Jesus was God alive on earth, the revelation of God is found in what Jesus said and did. God is revealed in Jesus himself rather than in rules and commandments that go back to the days of Moses.

Because of this, many Christians try to answer moral problems today by taking Jesus' life as an example of a human life lived perfectly. Therefore, to know the best way to behave in any situation, the question that many Christians ask themselves is, 'If Jesus were alive today, what would he do?'

Situation ethics

- To answer a moral problem correctly it is necessary to look at a specific case, one situation on its own, and make a judgement about that one situation.
- Rules like 'do not steal' and 'do not lie' work most of the time but in a crisis even these rules may have to be broken to do the right thing.
- Like Jesus, we should approach difficult moral situations by applying unconditional love or agape. This might mean showing mercy, kindness, forgiveness and a willingness to help others, even if they have done us wrong.

Joseph Fletcher (1905–1991)

A licence for permissiveness

- Taken on its own, 'love' is too ambiguous for solving moral problems.
- Used as the basis for making moral judgements, 'love' can easily turn into every person doing what they think is right in their own eyes – a licence for permissiveness.
- The guidance of the Church and long-established values should be taken seriously and not easily set aside.

'license of permissiveness'
Edwin Williams (1906–1994)

Selective quoting

- Using the Bible to find a quotation or a rule which seems to give an answer to a moral problem is suspect.
- Selective quoting involves quoting those parts of the Bible that provide the answer which fits existing assumptions or views.
- A more thorough study of the Bible may reveal a very different message that reflects the Bible as a whole, or parts of the Bible which may have more authority.

Unit 6 Things to do

Activity 5 Who stays in the lifeboat?

Joseph Fletcher describes a number of extreme situations which he believes challenge traditional views. One of them is a ship called the *William Brown*, which sank in 1841. This incident, Fletcher believes, challenges the claim that taking the life of an innocent person is always absolutely wrong.

In 1841 the *William Brown* struck an iceberg and had to be abandoned. One of the lifeboats had 41 people on board – 8 crew including the first mate and 33 passengers. This was twice the number the boat was designed to hold. After over 30 hours of being tossed about by stormy seas, the lifeboat had taken on so much water that it was in danger of sinking.

The boat was in danger of sinking.

The first mate, a man called Francis Rhodes, said that if the lifeboat was to stay afloat, people had to get off to lighten the load. The crew members threw 16 passengers – 14 men and 2 women – into the freezing water where they soon drowned. However, with fewer people on board, the lifeboat did not sink. Eventually it was picked up with 25 survivors on board. All 8 crew members survived and so did 17 passengers – 15 women and 2 men.

The crew members caused the death of 16 people but were they guilty of murder? Joseph Fletcher claims that, faced with a difficult choice, the crew did the right thing. What do you think?

a On a scale of 1 to 5, do you agree or disagree with Joseph Fletcher that the crew did the right thing? Explain your view.

1   2   3   4   5

Disagree with Joseph Fletcher, the crew did the **wrong** thing   Agree with Joseph Fletcher, the crew did the **right** thing

b Was there another way, perhaps a more loving way, in which the lifeboat problem should have been handled? Explain your answer.

c How might the problem have been solved by a believer in divine command theory who claimed that God's command is clear and says, 'You shall not kill.' Explain your answer.

Activity 6 Does rape justify abortion?

Dr Norman Geisler is a well-known Christian teacher and writer.

Unlike Joseph Fletcher, he argues that rape does not justify abortion. Part of his argument may be put like this:

The rape of the mother does not justify the murder of the child. Abortion does not take away the evil of the rape, it adds another evil. The rape problem is not solved by killing the baby. We should punish the guilty rapist, not the innocent baby. Should the mother not want the baby, there are lines of people waiting to adopt babies. Adoption, not abortion, is the better answer.

a In groups of two or three, discuss Norman Geisler's argument. Does Norman Geisler make a convincing case for his claim that rape is not a justification for abortion? Report back on the views expressed.

b Do you agree or disagree with the following statement?

The 'rape problem' is not the problem. The problem is the pregnancy.

c Does Norman Geisler's argument contain any words or phrases which might be considered to be misleading or which arouse an unnecessary emotional response? Or is Norman Geisler's choice of words entirely appropriate?

Dr Norman Geisler (1932–) His book *Christian Ethics* considers abortion, war, ecology and other ethical topics.

Activity 7 Some things are always wrong, or are they?

Opponents of situation ethics have claimed that some things are always wrong in all situations. Look at these four rules and choose one of them.

i Sex outside marriage is always wrong.	**ii** Stealing is always wrong.	**iii** Adultery is always wrong.	**iv** Civil partnerships are always wrong.

a Is the rule you have chosen always right or wrong? Explain your answer.

b Describe a situation to support your argument.

Activity 8 Selective quoting

Here are six Bible quotations. Choose one that you think is most in line with the teaching and actions of Jesus.

He who spares the rod hates his son, but he who loves him, will discipline him. (Proverbs Ch 13 v 24)

Life for life, eye for an eye, tooth for tooth. (Exodus Ch 21 v 23–24)

Who hits someone and kills him is to be put to death. (Exodus Ch 21 v 12)

Christ is supreme over every man, the husband is supreme over his wife, and God is supreme over Christ. (1 Corinthians Ch 11 v 3)

Do not ill-treat strangers who are living in your land. Treat them as you would a native among you, and you shall love them as you love yourself. (Leviticus Ch 19 v 33–34)

Honour your father and your mother that your days may be long in the land which the Lord your God gives you. (Exodus Ch 20 v 12)

a Justify your choice. Try to make your case as convincing as possible. Provide at least two pieces of evidence.

b Do you agree or disagree with the following statement? Explain your answer.

Using a stick to discipline a child is to follow what the Bible says.

Structuring an argument

What's wrong with sex before marriage? This is the question that Chris, aged 16, emails to Pastor Dennis Rupert, leader of the New Life Community Church in America. Pastor Rupert puts Chris's question to members of the church, particularly young members, and asks them to email their ideas. They all believe that sex before marriage is wrong and they give a variety of reasons.

The New Life Community Church in Virginia (www.new-life.net)

Six reasons why sex before marriage is wrong

1 It's not worth the risk of pregnancy or having a sexually transmitted disease.
2 Relationships that involve pre-marital sex fail.
3 It is true that sex before marriage will hurt you inside.
4 It will ultimately damage your sexual relationship with the one you do eventually marry.
5 It's a special gift that should not be wasted on just a love fling.
6 I think sex before marriage is wrong because the Bible tells us that it is.

Of the six reasons, only number six is based on God's law or teaching expressed in the Bible. The other five reasons are all consequences. Consequences are often used today to give a reason for saying something is right or wrong. Elizabeth Anscombe, thought by many to be one of the most outstanding modern British philosophers, called this **consequentialism**. She claimed that ethical theories like utilitarianism and situation ethics are not based on what God's law says. They are based on consequences.

Elizabeth Anscombe (1919–2001)
'The consequentialist has no footing on which to say 'This would be permissible, this not".'

A three-part structure

Although Elizabeth Anscombe was very critical of consequentialism, consequences are often used in moral discussions to form a basic three-part structure.

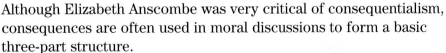

We've had a ride on this horse and cart argument before, haven't we, Mrs G?

We have, Matt. It came up in the first unit.

A three-part horse and cart argument has three parts: an opinion, a connective word or phrase and a reason. For example, if a person says, 'Sex before marriage is wrong because it's not worth the risk of pregnancy,' they are using a basic three-part structure. This can be shown in the form of a diagram.

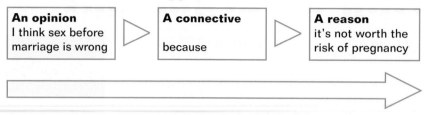

A line of reasoning

To be effective as an argument, the three parts have to fit together to make sense. They have to form a **line of reasoning**.

Activity 1 Making sense

a Here is an unfinished argument:

I think sex before marriage is wrong because …

Choose one of the following statements to complete it. Check that your argument makes sense and provides a line of reasoning. Explain why you chose your statement and why you rejected the other four.

i There is a danger that marriage will end in divorce.
ii There is a risk of getting a sexually transmitted disease.
iii It could result in fewer people going to church.
iv I'll be 16 soon anyway.
v It will cause a massive population explosion and millions will starve.

An opinion I think sex before marriage is wrong	▷	A connective because	▷	

Adding more reasons

Moral arguments which rely on a consequence can only be persuasive if the consequence is likely to happen. This means that a consequence has to be feasible. To try to make an argument more persuasive, the three-part structure is sometimes extended by adding more reasons, as shown in the diagram.

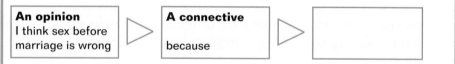

Persuasive moral argument

A moral argument isn't very persuasive if it's a series of consequences that are not very feasible. If each consequence is not very feasible, the argument is little more than a list of unconvincing reasons. Look at the sex before marriage argument in the box and read through it several times. Do you find it convincing? What would make it more convincing?

'What's so wrong with sex before marriage? All my friends have had sex with their girlfriends and they are in love. … If you love someone and you want to share your love, I think sex is not wrong'

(Chris, aged 16).

Sex before marriage argument

It is wrong to have sex before marriage. I think this because there is a risk that it may lead to pregnancy or to having a sexually transmitted disease (STD).

Another reason is that relationships which involve pre-marital sex often don't work out and fail. A person may feel that their partner is making a loving commitment, but they may find out that they are just being used, so they end up feeling really hurt inside. This may cause them to lose their own self-respect.

It is also possible that eventually when a person marries it may damage their relationship with their wife or husband. Their partner may resent the fact that they have had sex with another person and this may gnaw away at them and spoil the relationship.

Sex is a special gift which a person can only give once. Wasting that gift on a love fling means that a person can never give that special gift again. Sex before marriage is also wrong because the Bible tells us that it is.

Activity 2 Sex before marriage

a On a scale of 1 to 5, do you find the sex before marriage argument convincing or unconvincing? Explain your answer.

1   2   3   4   5

Unconvincing   Convincing

b How would a church in your local area answer the question, 'What's wrong with sex before marriage?' Write or email a local minister to try to find out about the views of members of the congregation. Report back your findings to the rest of the class.

Well, what's wrong with that argument, Mrs G? It has at least five reasons. That's an argument with belt and braces.

Not necessarily, Matt. An argument might contain many reasons, but they don't necessarily add up to make a persuasive argument.

Supportive evidence

A well-structured moral argument may identify only one consequence but if that one consequence is very feasible, then the argument can be very persuasive. Often the most persuasive moral arguments have **supportive evidence**. Supportive evidence is added to demonstrate that the consequence is feasible or, better still, very likely. An argument which uses reasons that are supported with **evidence** is called an **elaborated argument**.

The deterrent argument in the box contains an example of a reason that is supported by evidence. Is the evidence to support it good evidence?

The deterrent argument

I think it is right to bring back the death penalty.
If a person knows that the penalty for murder is death, that is likely to deter them from committing murder.

Evidence that this is true can be seen in what happened between 1965 and 1970. During those years the death penalty did not exist and yet murder went up by 125%. So I think there is an argument that the death penalty should be available.

Consequence

This part of the argument claims that there is a positive good which comes from having the death penalty – it deters people from murder. But is this true? To answer that question involves making a judgement about what people are like. Are murderers put off by the thought of death? Are most not deterred by the death penalty because they don't believe they will be caught? Are murderers so focused on what they want that most don't even think about a death penalty?

Evidence

This part of the argument provides evidence to support the above consequence. But part of making a moral judgement involves not simply taking evidence at face value. Evidence needs to be questioned and checked. For example, was it really a lack of any deterrent effect that caused murders to increase between 1965 and 1970? Were more guns and knives available and would that explain the rise in the number of murders? Have murders increased in countries where the death penalty has not been abolished?

Ann Widdecombe (1947–)
'If you can save life by having a death penalty … then I would maintain that there is an argument to be made.' Anne Widdecombe was the Home Office minister in charge of prisons from 1992 to 1997.

Ian Huntley was convicted of the murder of two children in 2003. Would the death penalty have deterred him from committing murder?

An elaborated argument

An argument which uses a three-part structure can be improved by using a structure that has **elaborated reasons**. This involves more than simply giving a reason or a list of reasons. Instead each reason is elaborated by attempting to justify or demonstrate the truth of that reason by using supportive evidence, as shown in the diagram.

An opinion	A connective	A reason	Evidence
The death penalty should be brought back	because	it deters people from murder.	The evidence that this is true can be seen in what happened between 1965 and 1970. During those years the death penalty did not exist and yet murder went up by 125%.

Opponents of the death penalty also use consequences elaborated with evidence to support their view. Here is an argument often used by those opposed to the death penalty; it's called the wrongful conviction argument.

The wrongful conviction argument

Judges and juries can make mistakes. Innocent people are wrongly found guilty of murder. If the death penalty were to exist, it is certain that innocent people would be wrongly convicted and wrongly put to death. In countries which do not have the death penalty, innocent people wrongly found guilty can later be released, pardoned and compensated. At least they are still alive. But if there is a death penalty, a pardon and compensation for their family will mean very little to the innocent person because they will be dead.

In 1950 Timothy Evans was hanged for a murder of which he was innocent. In 1952 Mahmood Mattan was also hanged for a murder he did not commit. In 1999 Sally Clarke was found guilty of murdering two of her own children, a crime she did not commit. Had the death penalty existed, she too would have been put to death. The death penalty takes the lives of guilty people but it also takes the lives of people that are innocent.

Timothy Evans was hanged for the murder of his daughter in 1950. He was pardoned in 1966.

David Davis has been shadow home secretary since 2003.

There are narrow circumstances for which the death penalty would be suitable. ... If you have got DNA evidence in multiple murders, there will be absolutely no doubt.

When we consider the plight of those who have been wrongly convicted, we cannot but be relieved that the death penalty was not available.

Moral decision making

Many people, religious or not religious, use consequences to help them decide moral issues. A great amount of moral decision making involves deciding what is the most likely consequence and weighing up the available evidence to help make the decision.

Does it all depend on consequences, Mrs G? Aren't there some things that are just forbidden? End of story!

That's certainly what Elizabeth Anscombe believed. The belief that something is wrong because it is against the law of God remains a powerful idea, Matt. It can be seen very clearly in Islamic ethics.

Islamic ethics

Although Islam uses consequences to explain and justify moral judgements, Islam is essentially a divine command theory of ethics. It claims that certain things are forbidden, or **haram**, whereas other things are obligatory and must be undertaken. Things which Muslims have to do are called **fard**. What is haram and what is fard does not depend on consequences or situations. Islam teaches that what is forbidden and what is obligatory are stated in a law which comes from God. That law is called the **shariah**.

The straight path

The Arabic word 'shariah' means 'the straight path' and appears over 30 times in the Qur'an, the holy book of Islam. It was originally used for the straight path taken by a person to find their way across the desert. The straight path connected the waterholes. Only by keeping to the shariah could a person hope to find those waterholes. Drifting off the path and losing the way to the waterholes meant certain death.

If a person comes off the straight path, they become morally lost.

Just as people needed to follow the shariah to find their way through the desert, so in Islam people need to follow shariah law to find their way through life.

The set of laws which make up the shariah are based on two main sources. The first source is the Qur'an. The second is the Sunnah, which is the words and actions of the Prophet Muhammad. However, there are other sources, including **qiyas** or analogy. This involves applying what the Qur'an and the Sunnah says to similar situations today. A fourth source is called **ijma**. This involves taking into account the consensus of the Muslim community.

Activity 3 The shariah

a Find out two things which are forbidden and two things which are obligatory according to shariah law.

b With a partner find out what you can about qiyas as a source of the shariah. Report back on your research. Give one example of how qiyas may be used to decide on a moral problem today.

Making things clear

In over 15 passages the Qur'an claims to be a book which makes things clear. Islam teaches that on the really important issues, no one can claim not to know what is right or wrong. Although some aspects of the shariah are disputed, there are core shariah laws that are undisputed and leave no doubt about what a true Muslim must do to live a good life. One of the best-known shariah laws is that every adult Muslim must give to the poor and needy. This obligatory law is called **zakat**.

'Charity is a necessity for every Muslim'
(The Prophet Muhammad, 570–632 CE).

'These are the verses of the Qur'an, a book that makes things clear'
(Surah 27 v 1).

Zakat is mentioned over 70 times in the Qur'an. It requires that after taking out what they need for themselves and for their family, every adult Muslim must give at least 2.5% of what remains to help the poor. Many Muslims think that one of Islam's great strengths is having very clear and feasible laws like this one.

The clear rule argument

Having clear rules that tell you exactly what you must do is one of the great strengths of Islam. The shariah provides moderate, feasible and very clear rules which remove any uncertainty. For example, uncertainty might arise over what to do about poverty in the world. If a Muslim has enough money to survive, should they help those who don't have enough? The shariah says very clearly that they must. However, uncertainty may still arise over how much to give. The shariah gives a very clear answer: 'After taking care of your own needs, at least 2.5% of what is left over must be given to help the poor.'

By following such clear instructions a Muslim can feel at peace, knowing that they have done what is required of them. They don't have to feel guilty and wonder whether they have done enough.

Persuasive moral argument

- A list of reasons, all of them unfeasible, does not make a persuasive moral argument.
- A well-structured moral argument may identify only one reason. If that reason is very feasible, then the argument can be persuasive.
- Evidence which supports a reason may be used to improve an argument so it becomes more persuasive. An argument which uses reasons supported in this way is called an elaborated argument.
- Example of a consequence: the death penalty means innocent people will be put to death.
- Example of evidence: Timothy Evans was hanged for a murder he did not commit.

Islamic ethics

- Islam teaches that what is 'right' and what is 'wrong' are made clear in a law which comes from God. Islamic ethics is based on divine command.
- The shariah, or straight path, makes clear what is forbidden and what is required. Drifting off the straight path is morally very dangerous.
- The shariah is based on two main sources, the Qur'an and the words and actions of the Prophet Muhammad.

If a person comes off the straight path, they become morally lost.

Clear moral rules

- Islam teaches that there are very clear, moderate and feasible moral rules which can be followed by everyone.
- Having very clear rules removes any sense of uncertainty about whether one is doing the right thing.
- Many Muslims describe Islam as a faith which gives peace of mind through knowing that they have submitted to God and have done what is required of them.

Islam teaches that giving 2.5% to the

Unit 7 Things to do

Activity 4 Elaborated moral arguments

Persuasive moral argument often uses a consequence or several consequences that are supported by evidence. Statements are frequently linked by connectives like these: because, so, otherwise, therefore.

a Arrange the five boxes to make an elaborated moral argument.

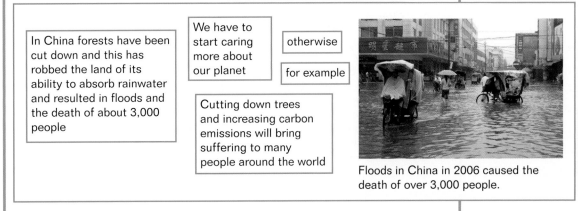

> In China forests have been cut down and this has robbed the land of its ability to absorb rainwater and resulted in floods and the death of about 3,000 people

> We have to start caring more about our planet

> otherwise

> for example

> Cutting down trees and increasing carbon emissions will bring suffering to many people around the world

Floods in China in 2006 caused the death of over 3,000 people.

b Arrange the five boxes to make an elaborated moral argument.

> Unless she is very careful and takes precautions, a girl can easily find herself with a baby and in many cases this will result in a life of hardship and poverty

> Evidence that this is true can be seen in the fact that

> because

> Young people should not have sex outside marriage

> In Britain women who gave birth as teenagers are twice as likely to be living in poverty, compared to those who wait until they are over 20

Some children are born to teenage mothers.

Activity 5 Persuasive writing

How can this argument about abortion be improved? Rewrite the answer to improve it and make it more persuasive.

Question
If a woman wants an abortion, no one has the right to stop her. Do you agree? Give reasons to show that you have thought about more than one point of view. Refer to religious arguments in your answer.

Answer
I do not agree. Abortion is wrong because all life is sacred. It goes against the will of God. Another reason is the baby may grow up to be an important scientist or musician. A third reason is that it says in the Bible, 'Do not kill.' The woman may regret what she has done and may feel bad about herself for many years. Some people say abortion isn't wrong because they say the woman has the right to choose and no one has the right to stop her. But I don't think she has the right to kill a baby. Because of these reasons, I do not agree. I think abortion is wrong.

How do you find the right answer to moral problems?

With a partner arrange the six triangles into a pyramid. At the top of the pyramid, put the view you agree with the most. Put your second and third choices underneath. At the base of the pyramid, put the three views you agree with the least. If you do not agree, say why you do not agree.

Give a reason for your first choice. If you do not really agree with any of these views, write a triangle of your own.

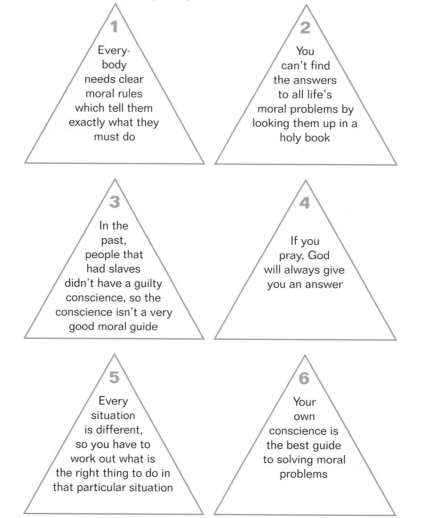

1 Every-body needs clear moral rules which tell them exactly what they must do

2 You can't find the answers to all life's moral problems by looking them up in a holy book

3 In the past, people that had slaves didn't have a guilty conscience, so the conscience isn't a very good moral guide

4 If you pray, God will always give you an answer

5 Every situation is different, so you have to work out what is the right thing to do in that particular situation

6 Your own conscience is the best guide to solving moral problems

Bill Gates, the founder of Microsoft, has given away nearly $30 billion to help the poorest people in the world. That is over one-third of his personal fortune.

Activity 7 How much should they give?

In groups of two or three, discuss this statement and report your views to the rest of the class.

Millionaires like pop stars, football players and top business people should give a lot more than 2.5% of their money every year to the poor.

Unit 8
Invalid arguments

We have seen that, over hundreds of years, different theories about ethics have been suggested. Yet because there are different theories and principles, it doesn't mean that our moral knowledge is a confused mess and we simply don't know. Important differences do exist about issues like experimenting on animals, war, genetic engineering, euthanasia and abortion. Nevertheless, there is a large amount of agreement on big issues like stealing, murder, being dishonest, curing the sick and giving help to people in need. This suggests there are some tricky grey areas that people disagree about. But there are also a lot of moral questions that are fairly black and white, so much so that we can recognise what is good and we have no problem knowing evil when we see it.

Activity 1 Odd one out

a Based on the morals of the four people pictured, who do you think is the odd one out? Explain your answer.

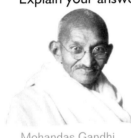
Mohandas Gandhi

Florence Nightingale

Adolf Hitler

Mother Teresa

On the big issues there is a lot of agreement about what is right and what is wrong.

b Discuss this claim with a partner. Report back on your discussion.

The nature of sophistry

Moral discussions are not always calm and thoughtful attempts to arrive at what is true. Some people see discussion and debate as an opportunity to be clever and to show off. They are not concerned about what is true or fair. For them, a moral discussion is a competition they have to win.

In ancient Greece, some of the greatest philosophers, like Plato and Aristotle, found themselves having discussions with people who did not want to know what was true. Like people in a wrestling match, they wanted to 'floor the opposition'. Such people were called **Sophists** and the practice of using clever but invalid arguments became known as **sophistry**. The Sophists' trick arguments sounded convincing but, after careful thought, turned out to be deceptive or just wrong.

Sophists of ancient Greece attempt to floor the opposition.

Even today, moral discussions are often littered with the tricks and flawed arguments of sophistry. Knowing these tricks and avoiding them can help improve the quality of moral discussions.

Sophists use many tricks and deceptions. Here are just a few.

The straw man

One of the tricks of a **sophist** is to give a false description of the views of their opponent. Often this description is highly exaggerated. The sophist then criticises that false description. This gives the impression that they have thoroughly criticised the opponent's views. In fact, they have done nothing of the sort. They have attacked a view their opponent did not have and they have sidestepped the issue.

The name 'straw man' comes from military training. To prepare for the joust, knights would train by attacking a straw dummy. The straw dummy looked like the enemy, but it was weak and defenceless and wasn't the real opposition at all.

Knights would train for the joust by attacking a straw dummy.

A straw man argument

Opponent: In order to tackle climate change, we all have to take responsibility and be more careful about how much energy we use.

Sophist: So you would have us all sitting in our homes in the dark hugging each other to keep warm. Everybody has to sell their cars and get a bike.

The red herring

The red herring is when the sophist avoids talking about the moral issue under discussion. Instead they try to divert the discussion onto another subject. This distracts their opponent and the argument becomes confused and fizzles out. Having not lost the argument, the sophist claims a victory.

The name 'red herring' has its origin in the training of hunting dogs. Hounds were trained to keep on the trail of a fox by following its scent. They learnt not to be distracted by the smell of a red herring dragged across the trail.

Hounds were trained with herrings not to be distracted from a scent.

A red herring argument

Why are we again debating the rights and wrongs of legalising cannabis? When you think of all the other important issues we should be discussing – crime, global warming, education – why are we wasting so much time on this subject?

The spurious relationship

The spurious relationship involves the sophist using false logic. Often the sophist will make at least two statements or premises that are true. The third statement, the conclusion, appears to follow from the two premises but is in fact false. However, it is difficult to spot why the conclusion is false, so the opponent is floored. The classic example is called the Hitler argument:

First premise: Hitler was an evil man. Second premise: Hitler loved dogs. Conclusion: People who love dogs are evil.

> Adolf Hitler was an evil man. Hitler loved dogs. So people who love dogs are evil.

The flaw in the argument is difficult to spot. The first premise 'Adolf Hitler was an evil man' and the second premise 'Hitler loved dogs' are both true statements. However, there is no logical connection between them, except that both are about Hitler. There is no logical connection between 'being evil' and 'loving dogs', it just happens to be true in the case of Hitler. It doesn't follow that every person who loves dogs must also be evil, so the relationship is a spurious relationship.

Activity 2 Valid or invalid?

Is the following argument valid or invalid? Discuss the argument in groups of two or three. Have a classroom vote using anonymous voting slips. Share your group discussion with the rest of the class.

War involves using violence. If a rapist attacked your sister, you would use violence to stop the attack. So you can have no objection to fighting in a war.

I've got a sophistry trick for you, Mrs G.

No, seriously, my sister does this all the time. It's called rubbish the opposition.

Is it one of your jokes, Matt?

Ah yes, Matt. A common ploy, usually called denigrating the opposition.

Denigrating the opponent

Similar to a red herring, denigrating the opposition is a tactic to divert attention away from the issue. The sophist avoids talking about the argument but instead talks about the arguer. The sophist may suggest some lack of knowledge or experience, or a moral failure which they claim disqualifies the opponent, making their view not worth listening to. Instead of judging what the opponent says on the merits of their argument, the argument is claimed to be false because the sophist has declared the opponent to be incapable of having a worthwhile opinion.

With a partner choose one of the statements (a) to (e) which you think is an invalid argument. Explain why you think it is invalid.

a The Americans killed innocent people with the atom bomb, so the Americans have no right to criticise the moral values of other people.

b Divorce is too easily available, so far too many people give up on marriage instead of trying to make it work.

c People who agree with abortion would allow a woman with any trivial problem she happens to come up with to abort her baby at any stage in the pregnancy. In fact, she doesn't really need a reason at all.

d All of the ten Sikh gurus were very good people. Guru Nanak was a Sikh guru and he was also a very religious man, so this shows that being religious makes people very good.

e Over 60% of the people in the survey said that they didn't agree with the war in Iraq, so there's your proof that the war was wrong.

Begging the question

When begging the question a sophist fails to prove the issue. Instead they assume the issue to be true and use that assumption in an earlier stage of the argument. As the issue is assumed in an earlier statement, it appears to be proved in the conclusion. Whether it really is true remains unanswered.

An example of begging the question

If you had hit your little brother, you would cover it up and say you hadn't done it. So the fact that you say you didn't do it proves that you did.

First premise: If you had hit your little brother, you would say, 'I didn't do it.' Second premise: You say that you didn't do it. Conclusion: You did do it.

The circular argument

A circular argument is similar to begging the question. The sophist fails to prove the issue but again assumes the issue to be true. They offer a reason or several reasons. However, these reasons do not provide a conclusion. They just lead back to where the argument started in the first place, which is with the unproven assumption.

For example, 'Stealing is wrong because you shouldn't do it' may at first look like a good reason. However, saying something is 'wrong' or that 'you shouldn't do it' or that 'it is bad' are really just ways of saying the same thing. The sophist is not establishing a proof or a justification but just repeating themselves in a slightly different way.

A circular argument

Stealing is wrong because you shouldn't do it

You shouldn't do it because stealing is bad

Bad things are wrong

The slippery slope argument

The slippery slope argument is often used in moral discussions. It is a variation on the straw man as it involves the sophist giving a misleading and exaggerated description, this time of what will happen in the future. The sophist claims that the opponent's views will lead at first to what looks like fairly harmless behaviour. The sophist then goes on to claim that this will lead to an unstoppable slide into behaviour which is very wrong.

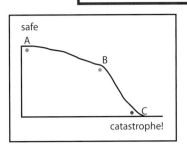

The slippery slope argument is not always sophistry. The slippery slope argument can be a valid argument if it can be shown that the chain of events leading to wrong behaviour is very likely. The slippery slope argument is invalid when the chain of events is exaggerated or can easily be prevented.

Activity 4 Slippery slope

a With a partner discuss the argument used by Natasha's mum. Do you think her argument is valid or invalid? Explain your answer.

b If Natasha's mum didn't draw a line at her spending time at the house of a friend, would it be safe to draw that line elsewhere?

Natasha: But Mum, why can't I go round to Becky's. I'll be back by nine.

Mum: I'm not having you spending time round your friend's house. I don't know what's going on there. You could be listening to that weird music, drinking, smoking … You could meet some boy there I don't know. Next thing you'll be hanging about in the streets with your mates and it'll be 'Can I go to a party?' Then you'll be telling me there's a boy you like, 'Can I see him?' Then after that …Well, you know the rest. I'm warning you, head off down that path and everything can go wrong.

Ethical thinking

Over the centuries it is possible to see many changes in moral attitudes. Racism was common in the past but now it is widely condemned. In the past, few people knew about the gap between rich and poor, and even fewer cared, but now many consider it a serious problem which has to be solved. Attitudes to women, children and animals have changed out of all recognition from what they were only a hundred years ago, although there still remains massive discrimination and abuse.

There are many reasons why these changes in moral attitudes have come about. One factor has been developments in moral and ethical thinking. Ethical thinking is still developing. In the field of ethics, new ideas and new arguments are continually put forward and scrutinised. By developing our ethical thinking, we can have a better understanding of the reasons which form the basis of our actions. It can help us to see the flaws in our own thinking and it can help us to see the bias and the assumptions which may influence our thinking and our actions. It can also help us to see more easily the inner structure of a moral argument and to distinguish between valid arguments and flawed arguments, so that we are not easily taken in.

Of course, this doesn't mean that the way people actually behave is steadily improving or that the world is becoming morally a better place. Knowing what is right and doing what is right are not the same thing. Nevertheless, understanding ethical thinking gives us the skills to see errors and avoid mistakes.

Unit 8 Summary

Sophistry

Greek sophists

- When a person uses sophistry they use clever but invalid arguments. A person who uses sophistry is known as a sophist.
- Moral discussions are often full of the tricks and flawed arguments of sophistry. Knowing these tricks and avoiding them can help to improve the quality of moral discussions.
- Sophistry is regarded as an unworthy way of arguing, as sophists are more interested in winning the argument than finding out what is true or fair.

Invalid arguments

- Straw man involves giving a false description of the opponent's view and criticising that false description.
- Red herring is an attempt to divert the discussion onto another subject.
- Spurious relationship involves drawing a false conclusion from two true statements.

Attacking a straw dummy

More invalid arguments

- Denigrating the opposition is finding fault with the arguer not with the argument.
- Begging the question assumes an issue and uses that assumption at an early stage in the argument so that it appears to be proved in the conclusion.
- Circular argument uses reasons which lead back to where the argument started in the first place.
- Slippery slope arguments claim that an action may appear harmless but that it is the start of an unstoppable slide into behaviour which is very wrong. Slippery slope arguments may be false or they may be true.

Things to do

Activity 5 What's wrong with euthanasia?

a   With a partner discuss the following argument against voluntary euthanasia. Do you agree or disagree with it? Explain your answer.

b   Is it important to draw a line against voluntary euthanasia? Would it be safe to draw a line at another point?

Voluntary euthanasia may sound okay. After all, what's wrong with helping a person who has only a few days of life left, to die in peace, free from pain? However, if we permit voluntary euthanasia, vulnerable people like the elderly could feel under pressure. They may feel like hangers-on who aren't wanted and that they should get out of the way.

If we go down the path towards allowing euthanasia, the consequences could be catastrophic. What starts off as voluntary euthanasia could become 'urging euthanasia' and then 'expected euthanasia' and finally 'compulsory euthanasia'. It is a morally dangerous path.

Michael Gove (1967–)
'All those of us concerned for the voiceless and vulnerable should … warn of the consequences of proceeding down this morally fraught path.' Michael Gove is the Conservative MP for Surrey Heath.

Activity 6 Two wrongs and appeal to the people

a   Find out about two more invalid arguments used by sophists – the appeal to the people and two wrongs make a right.

   Appeal to the people makes the invalid claim that if lots of people do it or believe in it, then it must be true or right. Here is an example:

Of course it's not wrong to try to get a penalty in football by diving. Everybody does it.

b   Make up your own example of appeal to the people or two wrongs makes a right.

Activity 7 Spotting invalid arguments

Look at the following arguments with a partner then choose one that you think is invalid. Explain why you think it is invalid.

a   Abortion is murder and murder is illegal, therefore abortion should be illegal.

b   In the nineteenth century, the British forced the selling of opium in China, which encouraged opium addiction, so the British have got no right to preach to the Chinese about human rights.

c You say we shouldn't provide aid to poor countries until they get rid of corruption. But what do you know about poverty? I bet you've never been poor. I bet you've never been hungry.

d There is such a thing as a just war. For example, most people believe that fighting against Hitler was a just war, so that goes to show that war can be just.

Activity 8 Guilty or not guilty?

You are the manager of a large supermarket store. You are told that a Mrs Miklos has been arrested by one of your security guards and is now sitting in your office. You go to your office and there you learn the following details.

Mrs Miklos is 76 years old. She was born in Hungary but has spent the past 30 years living in England. She has learnt little English but has lived a quiet life looking after her husband, on whom she has been almost completely dependent. Yesterday evening, Mrs Miklos' husband was taken ill and admitted to the local hospital. That morning Mrs Miklos, desperately worried, set off to visit her husband in hospital.

Mrs Miklos

While waiting at the bus stop, just outside the front door of the supermarket, Mrs Miklos decided to enter the supermarket and buy a small bottle of brandy as a gift for her husband and perhaps pick up a few groceries. She found the brandy and a tub of margarine, when through the glass doors of the shop she saw her bus pull up at the bus stop. Frightened that she would miss the bus, Mrs Miklos rushed out of the supermarket still holding the brandy and the tub of margarine. A few yards past the front door, she was arrested by Miss Dobson, one of the supermarket's security officers. Mrs Miklos offered to pay for the brandy and the margarine.

Head-office policy is to prosecute all cases of shoplifting. Miss Dobson says that she is prepared to give evidence in court that she arrested Mrs Miklos after observing her leaving the shop with goods she had not paid for. Your head of security advises you to call the police and say that the company wishes to press charges. Your deputy manager suggests that Mrs Miklos had no real intention to steal and advises you to let her go quietly.

a Get into groups of two or three then consider what the store manager should do about Mrs Miklos. Some groups should consider the problem using just one of these four theories:

   i   The Golden Rule
   ii The principle of greatest happiness
   iii Divine command theory
   iv Do the most loving thing possible.

b Report back to the rest of the class.

c Have a circle time where each person can say individually whether they think Mrs Miklos is guilty or not guilty of stealing and can explain their thoughts.

Who's who?

Anscombe, Elizabeth (1919–2001)

Elizabeth Anscombe is considered by many to be one of the most outstanding modern British philosophers. When she was at school, she converted to the Catholic faith and in adult life she rigorously defended the Catholic Church's opposition to contraception, abortion and homosexuality. She provided a famous criticism of what she called consequentialism.

Aquinas, St Thomas (c. 1225–1274)

Born in Italy, St Thomas Aquinas is considered by some people as one of the most important of all Christian thinkers. Often called the Doctor of the Church, his influence has been enormous, particularly in the Catholic Church. He adapted ideas from the Greek philosopher Aristotle to develop a Christian natural law theory of ethics. His natural law theory continues to influence moral discussions today, for example, in the claim that abortion interferes with nature and prevents the will of God.

Aristotle (384–322 BCE)

Along with Plato and Socrates, Aristotle is considered to be one of the three greatest philosophers of ancient Greece. He argued that right and wrong were not just local conventions which changed from place to place. He developed a natural law theory of ethics, arguing that by following natural laws, which were true everywhere, this would lead to the ultimate goal of human life, which was happiness.

Bentham, Jeremy (1748–1832)

Jeremy Bentham was an English lawyer and moral philosopher. He developed the ethical theory known as utilitarianism, which was based on the principle that what was morally good increased happiness and that what was morally bad increased suffering. He argued that this principle applied to living animals which felt pain, and he claimed that inflicting unnecessary suffering on animals was morally wrong.

Butler, Joseph (1692–1752)

Joseph Butler joined the Church of England as a young man. He rose through its ranks to become Bishop of Durham. He argued that conscience provided the basis for making moral decisions. He was sceptical about using consequences to decide what we should do and he believed that the consequences of our actions are often difficult to predict.

Confucius (551–479 BCE)

Regarded by many as a great and wise man, the Chinese thinker and philosopher Confucius has had a deep influence on life, particularly in China and Japan. Also regarded as the founder of Confucianism, he put great value on family life, respect for elders and daily moral behaviour. He taught an early version of the Golden Rule, which said, 'What one does not wish for oneself, one ought not to do to anyone else.'

Constant, Benjamin (1767–1830)

Benjamin Constant was born in Switzerland. His main interest was in politics. He believed that giving too much power to government was dangerous and that the power of governments had to be kept under control by a system of checks and balances. He criticised Immanuel Kant's claim that lying was always wrong and claimed that nobody had a right to be told the truth if they intended using that information to injure another person.

Davis, David (1948–)

David Davis is a prominent British politician who has sometimes expressed his views on contemporary moral issues. In 2003 he argued that the death penalty would be appropriate in very special circumstances, such as if a person was found guilty of several murders and where there was 'absolutely no doubt'.

Fletcher, Joseph (1905–1991)

Joseph Fletcher was an American professor of Christian ethics and a priest. He developed a controversial theory of Christian ethics called situation ethics. He believed it is wrong to treat rules as absolute, rigid rules which must never be broken. He argued that in any situation we should ask, 'What is the most loving thing possible in this situation?' He claimed this was how Jesus himself answered moral problems.

Gandhi, Mohandas (1869–1948)

More usually known as Mahatma Gandhi – Mahatma means 'Great Soul' – he was a political and spiritual leader in India in the twentieth century. He is particularly famous for his development of non-violent resistance, which he derived mainly from his Hindu faith in ahimsa 'non-violence'. Once, when talking about the principle of retaliation, he famously said, 'An eye for an eye makes the whole world blind.'

Geisler, Dr Norman (1932–)

Norman Geisler is an active Christian scholar and writer. He has written or co-authored over 60 books that explain and defend the Christian faith. He has written extensively on Christian ethics. In a discussion on abortion, he claimed that rape does not justify abortion on the grounds that abortion does not take away the evil of rape but instead adds another evil, that of abortion.

Gotama the Buddha (563–483 BCE)

Siddhattha Gotama was a spiritual teacher in ancient India and the founder of Buddhism. He rejected the idea that true fulfilment can be achieved by living a materialistic, self-indulgent life. Compassion, non-violence and respect for life feature strongly in his ethical teaching. He is credited with this version of the Golden Rule: 'Hurt not others in ways that you yourself would find hurtful.'

Hillel the Elder (c. 70 BCE to 10 CE)

Hillel the Elder was one of the most important of Jewish teachers or rabbis. He was still alive when Jesus was growing up. He devoted his life to the study of Jewish law. When asked to sum up his ethical teaching in a few words, he used this version of the Golden Rule: 'That which is hateful to you, do not do to your neighbour.'

Hitler, Adolf (1889–1945)

As leader of Germany from 1934 until his death in 1945, Adolf Hitler pursued an aggressive policy to expand German territory. His invasion of Poland in 1939 triggered World War II, which it is estimated led to the death of over 48 million people. His policy for dealing with 'the Jewish question' resulted in the death of 6 million Jews, many of whom were rounded up and deliberately murdered in death camps like Auschwitz. Hitler's name is often used in a demonstration of flawed logic such as this: 'Adolf Hitler was an evil man. Hitler loved dogs. So people who love dogs are evil.'

Jesus of Nazareth (c. 4 BCE to 30 CE)

Jesus of Nazareth is usually described as the founder of Christianity. He is the central figure in that faith. Often Jesus is called the Christ, a title which expresses the claim that his relationship with God is unique as the Messiah or as God incarnate, living on earth as a human. In his teaching, Jesus emphasised unconditional love for others and expecting nothing in return. He also taught a version of the Golden Rule: 'Treat others as you would like them to treat you.'

John Paul II, Pope (1920–2005)

Pope John Paul II reigned as Pope for more than 26 years until his death in 2005. He gave a clear lead on a number of contemporary moral issues, such as war, materialism and capitalism. In *Evangelium Vitae* 'The Gospel of Life', an official Catholic Church document, he very vigorously reinforced the Church's official objection to abortion, contraception and euthanasia and what John Paul called the 'culture of death'.

Kant, Immanuel (1724–1804)

Immanuel Kant spent his whole life in or near the East Prussian city of Königsberg. His life was extremely regular. He argued that a true moral act is not a means to an end. It is a moral duty undertaken for its own sake. He also believed that what was the right thing to do would be an action which could be universalised and so could be made into a rule which applied to everyone. He famously argued that lying was always wrong, even if a lie was used to misdirect a murderer from their victim.

Kennedy, John F (1917–1963)

Jack Kennedy, as he was often called, is the only Roman Catholic to have been elected president of the United States. In a number of speeches that are widely regarded as inspirational, he appealed to people to take moral responsibility and to join together to fight what he called the 'common enemies of man: tyranny, poverty, disease, and war itself'. He also famously challenged long-standing and deep-rooted racism and prejudice in America.

Kung, Hans (1928–)

Hans Kung is one of the most respected of Catholic scholars. However, his disagreement with the teaching of the Catholic Church resulted in the removal of his authority to teach Catholic theology in 1979. He has argued against the claim that there is a natural law which can help us to know what is right. He has also made a case for euthanasia, suggesting that it may be justified as it can help some people to die 'a dignified death'.

Mill, John Stuart (1806–1873)

John Stuart Mill was one of the leading supporters of utilitarianism in the nineteenth century. His belief was that doing good meant increasing general happiness, yet the happiness of women had been largely ignored. Women, particularly married women, were being treated unfairly and as people with virtually no rights. He also claimed that utilitarianism wasn't a godless doctrine and that it could be reconciled with belief in God.

Moses (c. 1300 BCE)

Moses was an early Hebrew religious leader thought to have lived over 3,000 years ago. He is credited with helping the Hebrew people to escape from slavery. Ethically he is most frequently associated with the story of God's revelation on Mount Sinai. During that revelation, Moses is described as receiving a large number of commandments from God, traditionally 613, probably the most famous of which are the Ten Commandments.

Muhammad the Prophet (570–632 CE)

For Muslims, Muhammad is the last and the most important of a long line of messengers or prophets of God. He is often known simply as the Prophet. The revelation given to Muhammad in the form of the Qur'an is central to Islamic ethical and religious thinking. The revelation of the Qur'an and the words and actions of Muhammad, known as the Sunnah, are the two main sources on which Islamic law is based.

Nightingale, Florence (1820–1910)

Born into a very well-to-do British family, Florence Nightingale chose to become a nurse, which was not considered a proper career for a respectable lady at that time. She pioneered modern nursing. During the Crimean War, Florence Nightingale and 38 volunteer nurses, who she had trained, cared for wounded soldiers in a British hospital in Scutari, now a suburb of Istanbul. She dramatically reduced death rates by improving the sanitary conditions in the hospital, and later she campaigned for better hospital sanitation.

Paul of Tarsus (10 BCE to 65 CE)

The letters of St Paul in the New Testament contain the earliest attempt to give an account of Christian principles and beliefs. His letters contain a great deal of moral guidance that continues to influence the views of many Christians today. Some of his ideas also contributed to the view that there is a natural moral law and that our own conscience can guide us about what is morally right.

Plato (427–347 BCE)

Together with Socrates and Aristotle, Plato is considered to be one of the three greatest philosophical thinkers of ancient Greece. Plato believed that what was 'good' didn't change from age to age but remained an unchanging truth. Rather like 'a cube must have six faces' is a permanent and unchanging truth, Plato thought that the idea of 'good' could not change; it was true now and forever. God could not change what was 'good', much as God could not change the inside angles of a triangle and make them add up to 170° not 180°.

Teresa, Mother (1910–1997)

A Roman Catholic nun who for over 40 years worked to help the poor, the sick and the dying in the city of Calcutta, now Kolkata. She set up an organisation called the Missionaries of Charity, which expanded her work into other countries. She was awarded a Nobel Peace Prize in 1979. In 1982 she rescued 37 children trapped inside a hospital by the fighting on the streets of Beirut.

Widdecombe, Ann (1947–)

Ann Widdecombe is a prominent politician who often discusses moral issues on television and radio. In 1993 she converted to the Catholic faith. She has consistently opposed fox-hunting, equal rights for gay people, abortion and use of the drug cannabis. In 2003 she suggested that if life can be saved by having a death penalty to deter murder, then an argument can be made for having the death penalty.

William of Ockham (c. 1285–1349)

William of Ockham was an English Franciscan friar. He is considered to be one of the best thinkers and philosophers of the fourteenth century. He took the premise 'God is Lord of everything' as his starting point and argued that logically this meant God must also be Lord of what is right and wrong. This line of thought resulted in a divine command theory of ethics, which seemed to claim that what is 'good' is whatever God says is 'good'.

Williams, Edwin (1906–1994)

Edwin Williams was a Christian minister and also the principal at the Bible College in Melbourne, Australia. He was interested in the differences that existed in the Christian faith and he wished to see the churches less divided. In 1972 he challenged Joseph Fletcher's ideas of situation ethics and claimed that using love as the basis of deciding right or wrong was too vague and provided a licence that permitted almost anything.

The useful word list

agape

Used in the New Testament to express giving kindness and help towards others without expecting anything back in return. It is often called unconditional love or Christian love.

ambiguous

Often used to describe a word or an idea that has more than one possible meaning. People may understand what is being said in different ways, which may lead to misunderstanding or confusion.

balanced argument

Often used to describe an argument in which both sides of the argument are explored, or perhaps more than two sides of the argument are explored. A balanced argument can also be a level-headed argument presented in a calm tone, showing good judgement and without making an excessive appeal to the emotions.

benevolent lie

A lie which, it is claimed, is the right thing to do as it will help bring about a good or will help avoid an evil. An example is lying to a murderer about where a person they want to kill is hiding. It is often called a noble lie.

categorical imperative

According to Immanuel Kant, for an action to be moral it has to be undertaken for its own sake and not because it will achieve some other end. A moral person does something because they believe it to be a moral duty and think it is the right thing to do in itself, not for any other reason.

consequentialism

First used by Elizabeth Anscombe in 1958 to describe moral thinking that used consequences or outcomes to judge what was right or wrong. She believed that words like 'right', 'wrong' and 'ought' did not make sense in an ethic based on consequences. They only made sense in an ethic based on laws, such as a divine command ethical system.

controversial

Used to describe an issue about which there is no agreement. A controversial moral issue is often debated and discussed but people continue to hold very different, indeed opposite views about what is good or bad.

divine command theory

An early theory of ethics which claims that God alone determines what is morally right or wrong. If God says something is wrong, then it is wrong as no other measure or standard exists that can be used to challenge what God has decided.

elaborated argument

Used to describe an argument which does not simply rely on giving reasons but which seeks to expand on or to firm up a reason, usually in the form of supportive evidence. An elaborated argument is a more sophisticated and persuasive argument compared to a simple three-part argument of opinion, connective and reason.

elaborated reasons

Reasons associated with an elaborated argument. They are reasons used in an argument in which an attempt has been made to make them more convincing, usually by providing supportive evidence.

Enlightenment, the

A period associated with eighteenth-century Europe when many traditional beliefs about religion, morals and how people should be governed were openly discussed and alternative ideas were proposed.

eros

A Greek word which refers to romantic, passionate and erotic love between a man and a woman. Not to be confused with Christian love or agape (q.v.) as taught by Jesus.

ethics

The study of what is right and wrong and how human beings should behave. Originally it referred not only to rules about what was right or wrong, but also to what virtues or qualities a person would have if they were to live an ethical life. Today the words 'ethical' and 'moral' have a similar meaning and are used interchangeably. It is derived from the Greek word ethike.

evidence

In the context of moral argument, the word 'evidence' is often used to mean supportive evidence (see elaborated reasons) which firms up and supports a reason. Evidence to support a reason may be in the form of statistical evidence. Evidence in the form of particular case examples, which give reality to a claim, often helps to make an argument more persuasive.

faith

Often when talking about religion or ethics, the word 'faith' means something similar to the word 'trust'. It often suggests a response that is not so much based on reasons which can make sense to others, but on certain feelings, emotions or beliefs which make sense to a person and so guide their behaviour. Some claim that all truths, including moral truths, are ultimately based on faith and that reason cannot lead to truth.

fard

An Arabic word for things that a Muslim has to do to be a good Muslim according to Islamic law. Examples are praying five times a day, giving zakat (q.v.) and fasting during the month of Ramadan.

Golden Rule, the

An ancient moral principle which rejects simple 'tit for tat' retaliation ethics and proposes that you should try to treat other people as you would like to be treated in those same circumstances. Stated in slightly different ways, the Golden Rule has been attributed to many of the world's great religious leaders and founders.

happiness principle, the

The claim that whatever increases happiness or reduces suffering is the way to decide what is right or wrong. The principle is particularly associated with the ideas of Jeremy Bentham, who called it the Principle of Utility.

haram

An Arabic word for things which are forbidden to all Muslims, according to Islamic law. For example, the drinking of alcohol and adultery are clearly forbidden in the Qur'an and are therefore forbidden in Islamic law.

humanism

Humanism comes in different forms but the common belief shared by all humanists is that the essential questions about life and existence can be answered without recourse to religious answers. One ancient humanistic tradition, which has its origin in the ideas of Aristotle, claims that by living according to natural law, humans may flourish and live a life of goodness in which they can find happiness and fulfilment.

hypothetical imperative

A phrase used by Immanuel Kant to describe things which a person believes they should do not for their own sake but as a means to achieve another end. Kant argued that a hypothetical imperative – doing something to achieve another end – could not be morally justified.

ijma

The consensus view held by the Islamic community and, according to some Islamic schools of law, a source of the shariah (q.v.). Ijma is based on the belief that although an individual Muslim might drift off the true path of Islam, it is not possible for the great majority of the Muslim community to drift off the straight path and so be in the wrong.

Law of Love, the

The Law of Love is derived from a saying associated with the words and actions of Jesus, particularly his statement at the Last Supper: 'Love one another. As I have loved you, so you must love one another.' The Law of Love requires people to show unconditional love or agape (q.v.).

lex talionis

A moral principle which rejects non-violence and unlimited violence but proposes returning violence with the same amount of violence. It is often called the law of retaliation (q.v.) or tit for tat.

logos

Used by the ancient Greeks to mean the fundamental order behind the universe. Aristotle used it to mean argument based on reason rather than argument based on mere passion or pathos (q.v.).

maxim

A fairly short statement, often no more than 10–25 words, that forms the basic moral rule which guides a person's behaviour. Often the word 'maxim' is used interchangeably with the word 'principle'. However, the word 'principle' is usually associated with having a worthy moral basis that takes account of other people, whereas a maxim may have little moral basis and may be entirely selfish or even cruel.

means to an end

The view that doing something that is wrong is justified if the end it achieves is good. Immanuel Kant argued that claiming an action to be morally justified because it was a means to an end was always a false argument.

monogamy

The custom that people have only one sexual partner and form an intimate, bonded relationship as a couple. Monogamy is most usually associated with monogamous marriage, which is a partnership between two people, typically a wife and a husband.

moral

Concerned with right and wrong conduct and how humans should behave. It most usually refers to laws and rules about what is right or wrong. Today the words 'moral' and 'ethical' have a similar meaning and are used almost interchangeably.

moral objectivism

The claim that what is morally right or wrong is not just about personal opinion. Certain ways of behaving are either right or wrong, and so justifying a moral view by saying 'It's what I happen to think' or 'That's my personal opinion' is claimed to make no sense. What is right and wrong is true, independent of human opinion, rather like knowing which is your left hand and which is your right hand cannot be altered by saying 'It's what I happen to think'.

moral relativism

The claim that what is right or wrong is just a matter of personal opinion, as right and wrong changes depending on culture and background. What might be wrong in the past might be right today. What is right for you might be wrong for someone else. Moral relativism claims that there are no permanent, absolute moral truths. It all just depends on what you happen to think.

motive

The cause a person has which results in them acting in a certain way. Immanuel Kant gave particular emphasis to the importance of motive when deciding if a way of behaving was moral or not. If a person's motive for giving money to a charity is so that they can brag about it later, Kant claimed they would not be acting in a moral way.

objective

When discussing morals, the word 'objective' usually expresses the claim that things are 'right' and things are 'wrong' in reality; they are not just a question of opinion or personal preference, or just what an individual happens to think. The word is often a shorthand way of claiming 'moral objectivism'.

pathos

Used by philosophers in ancient Greece to describe a way of making an argument persuasive by appealing to the audience's emotions rather than to their reason or logos (q.v.).

permissiveness

Derived from the word 'permitted' and associated with the idea that more things should be allowed or tolerated and not prevented on the grounds that they are morally wrong. People often use the word 'permissiveness' to criticise contemporary Western society when they claim that there are few moral codes and that far too many people just do what they want and take no notice of what is morally right.

philia

Used in ancient Greece to describe conditional love that involved mutual advantage such as the love between two friends who both gain from their friendship. The condition can be summed up like this: I'll help you but, when I need it, you'll help me.

premise

A statement which forms the basis of an argument that leads to a conclusion. It may be a piece of factual information or it may be a proposition that is generally thought to be true within a religious faith, such as 'God is Lord of everything'. For a conclusion to be proved, the premises of the argument must be true.

qiyas

Qiyas, or analogy, is a source of Islamic law used by some Islamic schools of law. It is based on seeing a likeness in two actions, one of which is forbidden in the Qur'an. It is then thought reasonable to conclude that the action it is very like should also be forbidden. For example, wine is forbidden in the Qur'an, so by analogy it is reasonable to suppose that drinking a Bacardi Breezer is also forbidden to Muslims.

reason

Thomas Aquinas used the word 'reason' in contrast to the word 'faith', and this is frequently how it is used today. In this sense, 'reason' refers to the claim that some knowledge, such as what is right and wrong, can be worked out independently of religious faith. This is done by using a logical line of reasoning that involves a series of statements, all of which follow on from each other to arrive at a conclusion.

retaliation

When a person who suffers an unkind act then inflicts an unkind act in return. It is sometimes known as 'returning evil with more evil' or 'do as you would be done by'. The level of hurt inflicted during retaliation may be similar to the level of the original hurt. If it is, it may be called proportionate retaliation.

shariah

An Arabic word for what is usually called Islamic law. The law is based mainly on the Qur'an and the words and actions of the Prophet Muhammad. For many Muslims, the shariah provides very clear, no-nonsense answers to what is right and wrong.

Silver Rule, the

A rule that says, 'Treat others as they wish to be treated.' It is related to the Golden Rule but is seen as a way of avoiding the criticism that the Golden Rule doesn't take into account different people's likes and dislikes.

situation ethics

An ethical theory mainly associated with Joseph Fletcher. It claims that no moral rule works perfectly in all situations, except the rule of love. Because of this, instead of simply following a rule, each situation has to be judged on its merits by asking, 'What is the most loving thing possible in this situation?'

sophist

A person who practises sophistry (q.v.).

sophistry

Using trick or false arguments to win a debate instead of using genuine arguments to find out what is true or fair.

Sophists

A group of thinkers in ancient Greece. Aristotle and others believed that Sophists used clever but invalid arguments.

subjective

When discussing morals, the word 'subjective' is usually used to express the claim that having a view about what is 'right' and 'wrong' has to do with the 'subject' that has that view. In other words, it has to do with an individual's personal preference, opinion or feeling. 'Right' and 'wrong', it is claimed, do not exist as a reality in the external, real world. A subjective view of morals is a form of moral relativism (q.v.).

supportive evidence

A feature of many persuasive moral arguments. It is added to demonstrate that what is often a consequence is feasible or very likely.

universalisation

A method of testing whether a way of behaving is moral or not. It supposes that the way of behaving is a law that applies to everybody and then sees if it will work. For example, to test whether stealing is moral, suppose that stealing is universalised by passing a law that allows people to steal, then see if that law will work. Universalisation is associated with the ideas of Immanuel Kant, but many people use it in today's moral discussions.

utilitarianism

An ethical theory which says that what is right or wrong is linked to whether an action increases happiness or increases suffering. It is particularly associated with the ideas of Jeremy Bentham and John Stuart Mill.

voluntary euthanasia

When a person says that they want to die and is then given help to die. The law in Holland allows voluntary euthanasia and the person's life must be ended by a doctor, not by a friend or relative. The request to the doctor must be clear, voluntary, carefully considered and repeated on several occasions.

white lie

An unimportant lie that is often used to be polite or tactful. Immanuel Kant believed that white lies are trivial and have no moral significance.

zakat

Giving wealth to help the poor and needy. As one of the Five Pillars of Islam, it is regarded as something which all Muslims must do in order to be a good Muslim, once their annual wealth exceeds a minimum level.